RACE and POLITICS

RACE and POLITICS

Ethnic minorities and the British political system

Muhammad Anwar

Tavistock Publications

LONDON and NEW YORK

First published in 1986 by
Tavistock Publications Ltd
11 New Fetter Lane, London EC4P 4EE

Published in the USA by
Tavistock Publications
in association with Methuen, Inc.
29 West 35th Street, New York NY 10001

Typeset by Scarborough Typesetting Services
and printed in Great Britain by
Richard Clay (The Chaucer Press) Ltd
Bungay, Suffolk

British Library Cataloguing in Publication Data
Anwar, Muhammad
   Race and politics: ethnic minorities
   and the British political system.
   1. Minorities – Great Britain – Political
   activity   2. Great Britain – Politics
   and government – 1979–
   I. Title
   306′.2   DA125.A1

ISBN 0-422-79840-1
ISBN 0-422-79850-9 Pbk

Library of Congress Cataloging in Publication Data
Anwar, Muhammad.
Race and Politics.
   (Social Science Paperbacks, 315)
   Bibliography: p.
   Includes index.
1. Minorities – Great Britain – Political activity.
2. Great Britain – Politics and government – 1979–
3. Great Britain – Race relations.
4. Great Britain – Ethnic relations.
I. Title.   II. Series.
DA125.A1A85   1986   305.8′00941   86–5715
ISBN 0-422-79840-1
ISBN 0-422-79850-9 (pbk.)

To my father
and in memory of my mother

Contents

Terminology

The term 'ethnic minority' is used throughout the book for those people whose origin is mainly from the New Commonwealth countries and Pakistan (NCWP). The two main groups of ethnic minorities in Britain are the Asians and the Afro-Caribbeans.

About the tables

1. Percentages are rounded to the nearest whole number and, therefore, some tables do not add up to 100.
2. A dash (–) is used for zero per cent but smaller than 1.00 per cent is shown by an asterisk (*).

Preface

Ethnic minorities are an integral part of British society. Their fullest involvement in all aspects of British public life is crucial if we are to create a society free of racial disadvantage and racial discrimination. I believe that, in addition to the economic progress of ethnic minorities, their integration into the political process is of fundamental importance. Furthermore, as we would like to see more professionals employed from the ethnic minorities, similarly there should be more 'decision-makers' from these communities.

However, the representation of ethnic minorities in the mainstream of British politics is still very small, though their participation in elections has increased recently. In the last few years, political parties have become more aware of the importance of the ethnic minority vote and the under-representation of ethnic minorities as elected people and party officials. Some efforts have already been made to encourage ethnic minorities to become members of the political parties, and ethnic minorities have responded to these efforts. But more needs to be done.

I believe that the integration of ethnic minorities into the political process requires their effective, not token, representation and involvement. They need to feel and participate fully in the decision-making process in order to feel that they are accepted as full citizens of this country.

Political involvement, power, and influence in British politics is important to highlight issues both through the ballot box and through politicians, party officials, committees, and civil servants. These channels are fundamental to influencing political decisions. In addition to voting at election times, the on-going and effective involvement of ethnic minorities in the political process is essential and should be beneficial to race relations generally and to help achieve equality of opportunity in our society, in particular. Continuous lobbying through pressure groups based

on specific issues or through other interest groups and voluntary ethnic
minority organizations is also important. The role of the media in this
context is important too: these pressure points are crucial for democracy
and for racial equality.

It was with the importance of the ethnic minorities in the political process
in mind that I monitored the participation of Asians in Rochdale in the
parliamentary by-election in 1972. Since that time, I have monitored all the
general elections and some local elections. These studies were undertaken
first on behalf of the Community Relations Commission (CRC) and now by
the Commission for Racial Equality (CRE).

No comprehensive work is published covering all aspects of the participation of ethnic minorities in the British political process. This book, based
on my research work in this field for the last thirteen years, will go some way
to filling that gap. It covers various aspects of the participation of ethnic
minorities in the political process. It also indicates the future role and
direction for their participation in the decision-making process. In
particular, it both looks at the response of the political parties and the
ethnic minorities in this context, and suggests ways to improve the
representation of ethnic minorities in this very important area.

My thanks are due, first, to several of my colleagues at the Commission
for Racial Equality and at Community Relations Councils for their help. I
am also grateful to many others outside the community relations field, in
particular to Dr Mich Le Lohe and John Hanvey.

Throughout the course of my research for this book I have been assisted
by several other individuals, including the respondents and the political
party officials, who freely gave their time. I am grateful to all these. Their
co-operation enabled me to produce this book, though they are not in any
way responsible for what it says.

I would also like to thank: Stanley Hope, MBE, Dr Abdul Rauf, JP,
Dr S. H. Syed, Daphne Poole, Ghulam Yasin, Zig Layton-Henry, David
Kohler, Mervyn Kohler, Professor Alan Little, Marian FitzGerald, Dr
Barry Kosmin, Paul Jennings, and many others who helped me at various
stages of my research for this book.

Finally, I must thank Deborah Spring of Tavistock Publications for
encouraging me to write this book and Elizabeth Saxby for her help in its
production.

Muhammad Anwar
August 1985

Introduction

Britain is now an established multi-racial and multi-cultural society. Over the last forty years people from the New Commonwealth countries and Pakistan whose colour differs from that of the majority indigenous population have exercised their right to come to this country. The estimated present-day number of these ethnic minorities is 2.6 million, or about 5 per cent of the total population of the UK (53 million). They can no longer be considered 'immigrants', since almost half of them are now British-born; many more came as children and have spent almost all their formative years in this country.

Over the centuries, Britain has received and absorbed a large number of immigrants from other countries. However, what makes the recent ethnic minorities different from and more visible than the earlier migrations is their colour. And it is because of this and their newness and different cultural backgrounds that the ethnic minorities face racial disadvantage and racial discrimination. It is a fact of daily life for many ethnic minorities. But despite these difficulties, ethnic minorities are playing an important role in British life.

The ethnic minorities are not evenly distributed throughout the country. They are mainly concentrated in inner-city and industrial areas, as most of them came to Britain as economic migrants. (See Chapter 1 for details.) For example, in 1981, 56 per cent were found in London and the South-East, 23 per cent in the Midlands, 16 per cent in the North and North-West, 4 per cent in the South-West and Wales, with relatively few (2 per cent) in Scotland. However, they are heavily concentrated within these regions in certain local wards and parliamentary constituencies, which makes them statistically significant in the political process. It is estimated that there are about 100 parliamentary constituencies where the ethnic minority population is more than 10 per cent.

Ethnic minorities in Britain have a right to vote as citizens of the UK or as Commonwealth citizens. How far have they exercised this right? What sort of response have they got from the political parties in this respect, and what is the overall importance of ethnic minorities in the political process? The answers to these questions, among others, are provided in this book.

Participation in the political process by the ethnic minorities is essential in achieving equality of opportunity. The process allows ethnic minorities to articulate their needs and to express their views on the policies of the political parties. This participation was monitored systematically for the first time in 1974 when the Community Relations Commission undertook research into the involvement of ethnic minorities in the general election in October of that year (Anwar and Kohler 1975). This research provided the benchmark against which the participation of ethnic minorities in parliamentary and local elections has been monitored since by the Commission for Racial Equality (Anwar 1980a, 1984a). These later studies demonstrated that ethnic minorities participated in these elections to a greater degree than had previously been recorded, an encouraging indication both of the extent to which they are becoming integrated into the mainstream of political life in this country and of their integration and involvement in the wider society.

However, there are also the 'pressure group' activities in which the ethnic minorities participate. This happens at individual as well as at group levels. Sometimes they get involved in direct political action, such as the 1980 and 1981 disturbances in some inner-city areas of Britain (Scarman 1981), or protests against unfair treatment and campaigns against racism and racist organizations. Political action in terms of marches and petitions also takes place against racial harassment, racial attacks, and deportations. These events get wide media coverage. Sometimes individual politicians and political parties are lobbied about these issues and political activists sometimes also make statements on these events and/or provide their support. This way, ethnic minorities regularly take political action and exercise political influence.

Lord Scarman's report about the 1981 street disturbances in Brixton and other areas and some other reports, in particular *Racial Disadvantage* produced by the Select Committee on Race and Immigration (HMSO 1981), and recently the Swann Committee report (HMSO 1985), have highlighted important issues. These reports have presented the government and the political parties with unique opportunities for tackling inner-city problems, eliminating racial disadvantage and discrimination, and improving race relations. But the government's response on the major issues in this field has been lukewarm, and statements made by various political parties have not been effectively translated into action.

One way to achieve political action by the political parties is to increase the number of members of ethnic minorities who are active in the decision-making process. This will help to achieve equal opportunity not only within the political parties but also outside them. As the white members of the political parties become more aware of the issues and the needs of ethnic minorities, they will thus formulate and implement more relevant policies.

The political parties should be in a position to show what they do and what is said on their members' behalf in the field of race relations; they should be determined to give effect to both the letter and the spirit of the Race Relations Act 1976. It is shown in this book how ethnic minorities and white electors react to the policies of the political parties concerning both race relations and other fields, and how they vote for them.

Political parties, in my view, cannot rely on ethnic minorities' support without giving something in return. The concentration of ethnic minorities in certain areas of Britain has maximized their statistical significance as voters. The political parties cannot afford to ignore this any longer.

The representation of ethnic minorities in the political process as decision-makers is not yet satisfactory. The House of Commons is still all-white. Some progress has been made at local council level, but it is very slow. In this book various aspects of the political participation of ethnic minorities are analysed objectively, because any objective political or 'sociological analysis by no means prevents political action; it prepares the way for it' (Rex and Tomlinson 1979). This book should be seen as a contribution in that context.

I hope that ethnic minorities will ultimately gain full acceptance and equal opportunity within the political process and, through it, in other walks of life. The involvement of ethnic minorities in this process is the genuine, long-term solution to racial disadvantage and discrimination at every level, to the conditions that breed despair and conflict in our society.

Chapter 1 deals with the immigration and settlement patterns of ethnic minorities. Chapter 2 describes the British electoral system and the civic position of ethnic minorities, and Chapter 3 examines 'race relations' issues in the political context. Chapter 4 analyses the registration and turnout patterns of different ethnic groups and Chapter 5 looks at the voting patterns of various ethnic groups. Chapters 6 and 7 describe the response of the political parties and ethnic minorities respectively to aspects of the political participation of ethnic minorities. Chapter 8 analyses the anti-ethnic minority vote by looking at the electoral performance of the National Front. Finally, Chapter 9 draws some conclusions about the participation of ethnic minorities in the political process and looks to the future.

1 Immigration and settlement patterns of ethnic minorities

It is a fact that most countries in the world today are plural in the sense that they consist of different social and ethnic groups. One recent phenomenon that has contributed to the formation of such 'plural' societies, particularly in the West, is the rapid economic development that followed the Second World War, and which attracted migrant workers. Since 1945 it is estimated that almost 30 million people, including their dependants, have entered the Western European countries as workers. In addition to these workers, many people returned from former colonies (like India and Africa) and after the war a large number of refugees also came to Western Europe. The population of Western Europe consequently increased by about 10 million between 1950 and 1957 (United Nations Economic Commission for Europe 1979: 272). The migration was principally from the less developed parts of Southern Europe, Asia, Africa, and the Caribbean countries to the highly developed parts of Western Europe.

It is estimated that in 1985 there are almost 16 million people of 'immigrant origin' in Western Europe, including Britain, who have migrated in large numbers from India, Pakistan, Bangladesh, Turkey, Africa, Morocco, Spain, Portugal, Yugoslavia, Italy, Greece, Indonesia, the West Indies, and Surinam, and in smaller numbers from other Third World countries. Although some migrated for political or religious reasons, an overwhelming majority migrated for economic reasons, i.e. in search of a better quality of life.

Over the centuries, Britain has received and absorbed large numbers of people from other countries and many Britons went abroad to the colonies as rulers, administrators, soldiers, business people, etc., to represent the Empire. But it is only in the last forty years that Britain has received in significant numbers from the former colonies workers whose colour differs from that of the indigenous population. The main sources of this immigration are the New Commonwealth countries (including Pakistan) of the Indian sub-continent and the West Indies. The estimated present-day number of ethnic minorities is about 5.0 per cent of the total population. Of these, almost 50 per cent are now British-born. Thus half of the ethnic minority population is not 'immigrant' but native-born British.

It will be useful to consider at this stage what distinguishes the migration from the New Commonwealth from other labour migrations to Britain. This migration has to be seen in the wider context; a study of previous labour migrations, the need for them, and reactions to them, puts into perspective the presence of ethnic minorities from the New Commonwealth.

Britain was one of the first countries to have large-scale labour migration in the nineteenth century. The Industrial Revolution rapidly absorbed the surplus of unemployed workers from the countryside and British employers also turned to Ireland (Thompson 1968: 469–85). In 1851 there were 727,326 Irish immigrants in Britain, making up 2.9 per cent of the population of England and Wales and 7.2 per cent of the population of Scotland (Jackson 1983: 11). They were concentrated in industrial cities like Liverpool, Manchester, and Glasgow, and soon came to form a high proportion of the labour force in unskilled textile occupations and in the building trades. Engels has described at great length the appalling conditions in which the Irish lived and has shown how they competed with the English workers for jobs and houses (Engels 1952: 9–94). Employers often kept Irish and English workers separate to avoid conflict at work. There was frequent discrimination with regard to housing and jobs; 'No Irish' signs were common in England during this period.

The next wave of immigrants to arrive in Britain in any significant numbers were Jews. Between 1875 and 1914, 120,000 Jews came to Britain from Eastern Europe, particularly Russia, to escape persecution there. Public reaction to these immigrants, who were poor and largely unskilled, was similar to that experienced by the Irish. The majority of them settled in the East End of London, where they were at the mercy of exploiting landlords and employers. Fear of competition for jobs and housing led to hostility from the local population. Mass demonstrations against immigration were organized, and the newcomers were accused of being the cause of most of society's ills. The campaign resulted in Britain's first restrictive legislation on immigration, the Aliens Act of 1905 and the Aliens Restriction Act of 1914 (Anwar 1979b: 3).

Immigration to Britain was on a considerably smaller scale during the inter-war period than it had been before the First World War, firstly because of the difficulty in finding employment for returning servicemen in the immediate post-war years and, later, because of the depressed state of the economy. Britain repatriated nearly all the workers recruited from the colonies during the war. But during the Second World War, British labour needs led to direct recruitment in Ireland and elsewhere by the Ministry of Labour. After the war, migration continued and estimates indicate a net Irish inflow of around 350,000 – or 30,000 per year – between 1946 and 1959 (Jackson 1963: 14). The rate of Irish migration slowed down in the 1960s.

Between 1946 and 1951, it is estimated that about 460,000 foreigners entered Britain. The largest group of these were the 115,000 Poles who came under the Polish resettlement scheme. They had been members of the Polish armed forces which fought under British command. Due to shop-floor opposition to their employment, it was very difficult for them to find jobs. Nevertheless, by 1950 most had found some sort of job. A certain number of former prisoners of war – Germans, Italians, and Ukrainians – were also allowed to settle in Britain (Isaac 1954). Furthermore, to overcome the labour shortage, the British Government carried out recruitment of European Voluntary Workers (EVWs). As many as 90,000 EVWs were recruited, mostly from refugee camps in Germany. They were engaged for three years for a specific job chosen by the Ministry of Labour and could be expelled at any time for misconduct (Isaac 1954: 182). Accidents or ill-health were also likely to lead to deportation (Foot 1965: 119). They were compelled to belong to a trades union, they could not be promoted over British workers, and they would be the first to be made redundant if such situations arose. Recruitment was confined mainly to single men or women, and only about 4,000 distressed relatives were admitted. Most of the male EVWs were directed to agriculture, textiles, heavy industry, and mining. There was also some recruitment of Italian workers at that time for specific industry.

The EVWs and other immigrants after the war, like the earlier immigrant groups to Britain, met with considerable hostility from British labour. The opposition of British workers to the employment of foreigners was strong enough to bring about their complete exclusion from some workplaces. However, all these workers were slowly absorbed into the labour market and more workers began to be needed in some sectors of industry. At the same time, British workers were emigrating to

the United States and the old Commonwealth countries, mainly to
Canada, Australia, and New Zealand.

Commonwealth citizens had free entry into Britain under the Commonwealth rules. With the colonial links and the knowledge about Britain of
several thousand soldiers and seamen from the West Indies and India
during the war, some of them decided to stay in Britain and others came
back to work after the war. They were initially welcomed by British
people as allies who had defended their national survival (Cabinet Papers
1950). However, the start of post-war mass migration was the arrival of
the *Empire Windrush* ship in June 1948. It docked at Tilbury with 492
immigrants from Jamaica aboard (Braham 1982). The process started
slowly but during the 1950s the number of immigrants from the West
Indies increased, reaching an annual rate of 30,000 in 1955 and 1956.
Although the Conservative party, elected to power in 1951, encouraged
both immigration and emigration, some concern was expressed about the
number of coloured immigrants. Nevertheless, the government's policy
was clear even in 1954, as Henry Hopkinson, Minister of State for the
Colonies, said:

> 'in a world in which restriction on personal movement and immigration
> have increased we can still take pride in the fact that a man can say
> *civis Britannicus sum* whatever his colour may be, and we take pride in
> the fact that he wants to and can come to the mother country.'
>
> (*Hansard*, 5 November 1954, Col. 827)

However, as pressure for immigration control grew, the Conservative
party changed from its policy of free entry for all Commonwealth citizens
to a policy of immigration control, publishing a bill on 1 November 1961
to restrict immigration.

As the pressure for and the debate on immigration control in Britain
started, more and more West Indians emigrated to beat the impending
ban. Between the beginning of 1961 and the middle of 1962, when the
Commonwealth Immigrants Act came into force, 98,000 persons
emigrated to Britain from the West Indies. Immigration from India and
Pakistan started later than that from the West Indies, but also reached a
very high level from 1960 onwards, as people tried to enter Britain while
there was still time (Rose *et al.* 1969: 55–90). The number of New
Commonwealth immigrants more than doubled in the inter-censal period
of 1951–61 from 256,000 to 541,000. Those who entered Britain before
the Commonwealth Immigrants Act of 1962 were predominantly econ-
omically active persons. They included a high proportion of women

among the West Indians, while the overwhelming majority of the Indians and Pakistanis were men. The voucher system under the Act gave the opportunity for those who were already here to arrange jobs and vouchers for their relatives and friends. This increased the element of sponsorship and patronage. Dependants of those already in Britain were allowed to come without vouchers. Between July 1962 and December 1968, only 77,966 voucher holders were admitted, compared with 257,220 dependants (Deakin 1970: 52).

I would argue that the 1962 Act had a decisive effect on the pattern of migration. It turned a movement of workers, many of whom were probably only interested in staying temporarily, into a relatively permanent immigration of families, and the voucher system initially reinforced kinship and friendship bonds and therefore reinforced the pattern of settlement. The net immigration from the West Indies, India, and Pakistan between 1955 and 1968 was 669,640 (Anwar 1979b).

The number of people arriving for settlement from all the New Commonwealth countries in 1969–77 was 318,521. Of these, 259,646 came as dependants and only 58,875 were male workers. This shows a drastic decline in the number of immigrants entering as workers from the New Commonwealth countries. This pattern of decline for male workers, and now of dependants as well, has been continued. For example, the 'primary' immigration, i.e. men accepted here for settlement on arrival – 17,900 in 1972 – was reduced to a trickle – 1,700 – in 1982 and is now mainly confined to professionals still in short supply in this country. Even the immigration of dependant women and children was more than halved from about 50,000 in 1972 to about 23,000 in 1982. Total immigration from the New Commonwealth countries and Pakistan (NCWP) has declined sharply from 68,000 in 1972 to 24,800 in 1984. It is interesting to note that this is less than half the total of all immigration to this country: 51,000 in 1984 (including whites).[1] On the basis of these figures it is therefore fair to say that large-scale immigration from the NCWP countries is now over. Between 1971 and 1983 more people had left Britain than had entered it. Overall, the net loss of population by migration during this period was 465,000, mainly as a result of emigration to Australia, Canada, New Zealand, the United States, South Africa, and the EEC countries.

British public reaction to immigration from the New Commonwealth during these years was the same as it had been to the previous waves of migrations. Signs such as 'All blacks go home' and 'Send them back' were quite common. 'Paki-bashing' and other anti-immigrant demonstrations and activities are still taking place. The British Campaign to Stop Immigration and the actions of the National Front have been prime examples in this context. Racial attacks and racial harassment are facts of life for many ethnic minorities in the 1980s.[2]

However, looking at the occupations which most of the immigrants have taken up, we can see that the labour migration from other countries to Britain was an important factor in the post-war expansion of industries and services; also that almost half of the ethnic minority population is now British-born and is not 'immigrant'. Furthermore, Britain still depends on its ethnic minority workers' contribution to the economy.

Settlement patterns

Like the previous waves of migration to Britain, the ethnic minorities (mainly of the NCWP origin) have settled in industrial areas where there are job opportunities. This applied both to those who initially had freedom of movement and to those who came through government and employers' recruitment efforts. It means that the ethnic minority population is not distributed throughout the country in the same way as the white population. A large number of members of the ethnic minorities live in a small number of local authority areas and there is further concentration of them in a small number of electoral wards. This is fundamental to their 'statistical' significance as electors in the areas of their concentration.

The 1981 census shows that the ethnic minority population was a little over 2.2 million, which is 4.2 per cent of the total population.[3] By using the 1981 census as a base (the latest systematic figures about the geographical distribution available) we find that most of the ethnic minorities are to be found in the South-East (56 per cent), especially in the Greater London area, the Midlands (23 per cent), the North and the North-West (16 per cent), and the remainder (5 per cent) in the South-West, Wales, and (relatively few) in Scotland (in the Central Clydeside conurbation, mainly in Glasgow, and also in Edinburgh). The contrast between the general population in Greater London and the South-East (31 per cent) and the ethnic minority population (56 per cent) is particularly marked (see *Table 1*).

The 1981 census figures show that of the 2.2 million ethnic minority population, an estimated 1.2 million (55 per cent) are of Asian origin, about 0.55 million (25 per cent) are of Afro-Caribbean origin, and the remaining 20 per cent of British ethnic minorities have their origin in

Table 1 *Persons resident in private households, total population and those with head of household born in the New Commonwealth and Pakistan: Regions*

	Total population		NCWP population		NCWP % of total population
	No.	%	No.	%	
Scotland	4,954,328	(9.4)	46,188	(2.1)	0.9
North, Yorkshire and Humberside and North-West	14,075,451	(26.7)	349,286	(15.8)	2.5
Midlands and East Anglia	10,598,267	(20.1)	495,943	(22.5)	4.7
South-East					
Greater London	6,492,642	(12.3)	945,148	(42.8)	14.6
Remainder	9,759,911	(18.5)	282,606	(12.8)	2.9
South-West and Wales	6,879,732	(13.0)	88,074	(4.0)	1.3
Total	52,760,331	(100)	2,207,245	(100)	4.2

Source: Registrar General, Scotland and OPCS, Census 1981: National Report, Great Britain, part 1, Table 11, HMSO, 1983.

South-East Asia, the Mediterranean, and other parts of the New Commonwealth (see *Table 2*).

Further analysis of the census data shows that Afro-Caribbeans are highly concentrated in the South-East (65 per cent) with over half (56 per cent) in the Greater London area. Nearly half (48 per cent) of those of Indian origin were also living in the South-East; as were 57 per cent of Bangladeshis and 65 per cent of East African Asians, but only 31 per cent of Pakistanis. Almost two-thirds of the total population of Pakistani origin live in the conurbations of the West Midlands (22 per cent), Yorkshire and Humberside (21 per cent), and the North-West (16 per cent). The settlement pattern of Pakistanis in these regions, in some cities and towns within these areas and, on a smaller scale, within towns on the basis of · their home origin, is not a chance phenomenon. It came about as a result of the active kin-friend 'chain migration' (Anwar 1979b). But generally the settlement patterns of ethnic minorities were clearly determined by the availability of work in different areas, as most of them initially came as economic migrants.

Migration from the New Commonwealth countries and Pakistan to Britain was initially predominantly male. The balance of the sexes among Afro-Caribbeans is now almost the same as for the general population but there is still a relatively high ratio of men to women Asians, particularly among Pakistanis and Bangladeshis. However, with the arrival of

Table 2 Persons resident in private households with head of household born in the New Commonwealth and Pakistan (NCWP) by country of origin

	Caribbean	India	Pakistan	Bangladesh	East Africa	Far East	Mediter- ranean	Remainder	Total NCWP
All persons									
born inside UK	273,558	261,206	118,252	16,939	48,673	39,742	79,315	57,907	895,592
born outside UK	272,186	412,498	177,209	47,622	132,648	80,381	90,763	98,346	1,311,653
Total persons	545,744	673,704	295,461	64,561	181,321	120,123	170,078	156,253	2,207,245
	(24.7)	(30.5)	(13.4)	(2.9)	(8.2)	(5.4)	(7.7)	(7.2)	(100)

Note: Figures in brackets = Great Britain %.

Source: OPCS, Census 1981.

dependants from the Indian sub-continent, the Asian sex ratio is moving towards that of the rest of the population. For example, the figures between 1961 (82 per cent males) and 1982 (58 per cent males) for Pakistanis show that the ratio of men to women is changing more rapidly (Anwar 1984b: 12). The sex ratio for the general population, according to the 1981 census, was 48 per cent males and 52 per cent females.

The ethnic minority population is much younger than the white population. It has far fewer older people aged 65 plus (less than 3 per cent compared with 12 per cent for the total population). More than half of the population of Asian and West Indian origin, compared with about 35 per cent of the general population, is under 25. Almost 40 per cent of Asians are under 16 years old compared with 30 per cent of West Indians and only 22 per cent of the general population (OPCS 1981 Census: Table 3). There are relatively more children among the ethnic minority population than the general population, as shown in *Table 3*. (Because of the sex ratio differences between different ethnic groups, a table for *males* only is used.)

One important development in this context is the increasing number of ethnic minority children born and educated in this country. According to the 1981 census, almost 93 per cent of ethnic minority children aged 0–4 and 81 per cent of those aged 5–15 were born in Britain. The majority, 60 per cent, aged 16–19, were also born in this country. Altogether, it is estimated that over 40 per cent of ethnic minorities in Britain were born in this country, although there are differences between the two main ethnic minority groups, the West Indians and the Asians. While over half of the West Indians were born in this country, the figure for Asians was under 40 per cent (Brown 1984: 17). One important reason for this difference is the different timing of the principal migration periods for the two groups, as mentioned above.

Most of the original ethnic minorities who came to Britain were economic migrants, and their position in the labour market is a fundamental aspect of their position in British society. The type of work available to them not merely governs their incomes, it also helps to determine in which areas they settle, where their children go to school, how they interact with the indigenous labour force and population generally, their chances of participation in civic life, and their overall status in society. If ethnic minorities are granted access only to a limited range of occupations upon arrival, there will be concentrations in certain industrial sectors and factories and consequently, depending on their locations, there will be concentrations in certain towns, cities, and regions.

Table 3 *Age distribution of males by country of origin*

Males age	Total male population		Total NCWP males		Caribbean		India		Pakistan		Bangladesh		East Africa		Remainder	
	No.	(%)	No.	(%)	No.	(%)	No.	(%)	No.	(%)	No.	(%)	No.	(%)	No.	(%)
0–4	1,646,866	(6.4)	121,107	(10.7)	18,462	(7.0)	34,686	(10.2)	28,106	(17.4)	5,945	(14.9)	11,546	(12.6)	22,362	(9.7)
5–15	4,450,302	(17.3)	258,110	(22.9)	67,757	(25.6)	79,663	(23.4)	43,176	(26.8)	8,833	(22.1)	15,787	(17.2)	42,894	(18.7)
16–19	1,768,867	(6.9)	95,852	(8.5)	35,568	(13.4)	26,726	(7.9)	8,645	(5.4)	2,489	(6.2)	5,645	(6.1)	16,779	(7.3)
20–29	3,735,081	(14.5)	212,517	(18.8)	37,119	(14.0)	59,803	(17.6)	29,924	(18.6)	6,604	(16.5)	24,149	(26.3)	54,918	(23.9)
30–44	5,209,181	(20.3)	220,936	(19.5)	42,986	(16.2)	66,179	(19.4)	26,138	(16.2)	7,706	(19.3)	23,758	(25.8)	54,169	(23.6)
45–64	5,797,328	(22.6)	189,475	(16.8)	57,814	(21.8)	59,524	(17.5)	23,127	(14.3)	7,996	(20.0)	9,207	(10.0)	31,807	(13.9)
65+	3,073,799	(12.0)	30,718	(2.8)	5,530	(2.0)	14,074	(4.0)	2,166	(1.3)	420	(1.0)	1,845	(2.0)	6,683	(2.9)
All ages	25,681,424	(100)	1,128,715	(100)	265,236	(100)	340,655	(100)	161,282	(100)	39,993	(100)	91,993	(100)	229,612	(100)

Note: Figures in brackets = Great Britain %.

Source: OPCS, Census 1981: Country of Birth, Great Britain, Table 3, HMSO, 1983.

At least two recent surveys give us a depressing picture of the economic lives of Afro-Caribbeans and Asians (Anwar 1982b; Brown 1984: 150–83). They are more likely than white people to be unemployed, and those who are working generally have jobs with lower pay and lower status than those of white workers.

Over the last three decades there has been little change in the types of jobs done by the majority population and by the ethnic minorities, while their unemployment rates have sharply diverged, especially among young people. Research evidence on employment shows that a number of factors govern the pattern of 'poor' jobs among the ethnic minorities, including their newness, the different educational backgrounds of workers from different ethnic groups, the higher incidence of the lack of fluency in English among Asian workers, different residential patterns for the majorities of white and ethnic minority workers, an ethnic minority labour market which seems to be in some respects quite different from that of white workers, and widespread racial discrimination both direct and indirect (CRE Annual Reports 1981–84 and Brown 1984: 293). An overwhelming majority of ethnic minorities are semi-skilled or unskilled workers. The majority of them are employed in manufacturing industries. Ethnic minorities are under-represented in the distribution trade, which forms the largest single area of employment for the total population of Britain. But at the same time, recent trends show that the number of self-employed Asians is increasing at a faster rate than among the indigenous population.

In the housing field, as far as the overall tenure pattern is concerned, there are differences between different ethnic groups. For example, over 70 per cent of Asians are owner-occupiers, compared with just over 40 per cent of West Indians and about 60 per cent of whites. Owner-occupation among Asians in some areas outside London is as high as 90 per cent. But as most of them live in inner-city areas the quality of their housing is very poor. They face the acute problems of the inner cities and these lead them to suffer an overall pattern of racial disadvantage in housing, in both the private and public sectors (CRE 1984).

Another relevant factor is the language difficulty encountered by some Asians and other groups like the Chinese and those who come here from Cyprus. A recent survey showed that a substantial proportion of the adult Asian population, a fifth of Asian men and nearly half of Asian women, speak English 'slightly or not at all'. There is a very strong correlation with age. For example, over half of Asian adults under 25, and 90 per cent of those born in Britain, speak English fluently (Brown 1984: 128–30).

As young Asians grow up in Britain the proportion of fluent English-speaking adults rises, but older people are not helped in this direction: no doubt the concentration of Asians in certain workplaces, the formation of ethnic work groups and the type of jobs they do, together with the fact that the majority of them are on shift work, are all contributory factors in inhibiting the process of learning English, as the need to use English for communication is minimized (Anwar 1979b: 105–24). However, in addition to the employment field, the lack of fluency in English restricts participation in other walks of life, especially in the civic life of the society. Despite their linguistic disadvantage, however, Asians do participate in great numbers at elections with the assistance of leaders who help to organize and mobilize them (Anwar 1979b: 136–57).

2 The civic position of ethnic minorities and the electoral system

The participation of ethnic minorities in the British political process is an important indication of their involvement in the society. Because of the historical links of ethnic minorities from the New Commonwealth and Pakistan with Britain they, as British and Commonwealth citizens living in this country, have a legal right to participate fully in politics. This includes the right to vote and to be a candidate in elections. However, such participation is not new. Three MPs from the Indian subcontinent (all Parsees) had been elected to the House of Commons before the Second World War. The first, Dadabhai Naoroji, was elected as long ago as 1892 as a Liberal with a majority of five at Finsbury Central. The second, Sir Mancherjee Bhownagree, was twice elected as a Conservative for Bethnal Green North East in 1895 and 1900. The third, Shapurji Saklatvala, was twice elected for Battersea North, as a Labour candidate in 1922 and as a Communist in 1924. In the House of Lords, there was one member from the Indian subcontinent, Lord Sinha of Raipur (1863–1928). However, since the Second World War there have been no MPs from the ethnic minorities, although there have been three members of the House of Lords, Lords Constantine, Pitt, and Chitnis. There have been a number of parliamentary candidates who belonged to the ethnic minorities. These included both those who have stood as candidates for the main political parties and those who have come forward for the minor political parties or have stood as independent candidates.

It was during the 1964 general election, and particularly in Smethwick, that immigration and race emerged as major factors in British politics. Their emergence merely reinforced the already narrow focus on the impact of the presence of ethnic minorities on the general electoral behaviour of the population. Two developments in particular had brought the issue of ethnic minorities into the open. The first was the race riots in

Nottingham and Notting Hill in West London in August and September of 1958, which drew the public's attention to their presence.[1] The second was the formation of the Southall Residents' Association in September 1963 to protest against the increasing number of Indians settling down in the borough and the presence of their children in the schools.

At the time of the 1964 general election in Smethwick, Peter Griffiths, the Conservative party candidate, supported slogans like 'If you want a nigger neighbour, vote Labour' (*The Times*, 9 March 1964). There were other areas where race and immigration were made election issues, notably Southall, where the British National party candidate received 3,410 votes, Perry Barr in Birmingham where the Birmingham Immigration Control Association helped the Conservative candidate, and Eton and Slough where Fenner Brockway, the Labour candidate and a campaigner against racial discrimination, lost his seat (Brockway, in *Tribune* 23 October 1964). These results, and particularly the one in Smethwick, showed that racial prejudice could be effectively exploited for electoral advantage. Patrick Gordon-Walker, the Shadow Foreign Secretary, was dramatically unseated by the Conservative candidate, Peter Griffiths. Although the Labour party was returned to office, the Smethwick result was against the national swing and a blow to race relations.

The Labour party was already being cautious on the immigration issue, as was reflected in its manifesto for the 1964 general election:

'A Labour government will legislate against racial discrimination and incitement in public places and give special help to local authorities in areas where immigrants have settled. Labour accepts that the number of immigrants entering the United Kingdom must be limited. Until a satisfactory agreement covering this can be negotiated with the Commonwealth, a Labour government will retain immigration control.'

(Labour Party 1964)

After the Smethwick result, Harold Wilson, the new Prime Minister, attacked Peter Griffiths on the first day of the new parliament. He asked Sir Alec Douglas-Home to repudiate the victor of Smethwick who 'until a further general election restores him to oblivion, will serve his term here as a parliamentary leper' (*Hansard*, 3 November 1964: Col. 71). Other Labour speakers attacked Peter Griffiths as well. However, it was clear that after this, the Labour government was in favour of effective immigration control, as the Home Secretary, Sir Frank Soskice, told the House on 17 November 1964. The Labour party appeared to feel that the immigration issue could be a vote-loser for the Labour party. As Crossman wrote in his diaries, 'immigration can be the greatest potential vote-loser for the Labour party if we are seen to be permitting a flood of immigrants to come in and blight the central cities' (Crossman 1975: 150). With a majority of only five, the Labour government was being very careful on the immigration issue. It had decided to try to achieve some form of bi-partisan agreement with the Conservatives so that the next election could be fought on the more secure and traditional grounds of economics and class (Katznelson 1973).

The Conservative leadership was calling now for tougher immigration controls and the Labour party appeared to be responding when the Home Secretary announced in the House of Commons that he was tightening the immigration regulations governing the entry of dependent relatives. He also sought powers to deport illegal immigrants as, he argued, evasion of the immigration rules was taking place on a large scale (Layton-Henry 1984 and *Hansard*, 4 February 1965: Col. 1284–5). The Labour party took other steps to meet its manifesto commitments. For example, on 9 March 1965, the Prime Minister announced the appointment of Maurice Foley, MP, Under-Secretary of State at the Department of Economic Affairs, as the minister responsible for the government's policy for co-ordinating action to encourage assimilation and better community relations, especially in the big cities. The Prime Minister also announced that the government would fulfil its pledge to introduce a bill forbidding racial discrimination and would legislate to provide penalties against incitement to racial hatred. As far as immigration was concerned, he announced that there would be a fresh examination of the machinery of control because of the problems of evasion and a high-level mission would be sent to discuss the problems of control with the relevant Commonwealth governments. This mission was headed by Lord Mountbatten and visited some 'sending' countries. Not only was Mountbatten to return empty handed from his tour, but he was not even allowed to visit Pakistan, one of the major sending countries during that period (Layton-Henry 1984: 62).

However, in all the debates on immigration and community relations during 1965 and early 1966, it was confirmed by the Labour government that the country needed effective control on numbers coming from the New Commonwealth countries, thus expressing the bi-partisan consensus on this issue. Then, in August 1965, the White Paper *Immigration from the Commonwealth* was published which outlined the government's future policy on this issue and the policy to help - integration. The response to the White Paper was mixed. Crossman wrote, 'No wonder all the liberal papers have been bitterly attacking us. Nevertheless I am convinced that if we hadn't done this we would have been faced with certain electoral defeat in the West Midlands and the South-East' (Crossman 1975: 299). This frank confession by Crossman shows that the Labour party did not want to lose votes because of this issue in the next general election and this way, by its actions, it violated some of its liberal principles.

The next general election was held in March 1966 and Labour came back into power with an overall majority of 100 seats. Neither race nor immigration became election issues because Edward Heath, leader of the opposition, did not allow Conservative candidates to exploit these issues during their election campaigns.

The Labour party won the seats it lost where the race issue had been used in 1964. But there were signs that the increased registration of ethnic minorities as electors and their increased turnout in that election had helped Labour seats in the areas of ethnic minority settlement (Studlar 1978). The 1964 and 1966 general elections were the turning points as far as the political participation of ethnic minorities in this country is concerned, partly because they had responded to the attention that had been focused on immigration and race issues by politicians and anti-immigrant organizations, and partly a genuine effort was made on their part to express through the ballot box their opinions about the policies of the political parties.

What has been the impact of ethnic minority voters upon British politics? Are there many such voters? Do they occupy a strategic position in the elections, especially in inner-city marginal constituencies? The answer to the last question is yes. There are several reasons for this. First, ethnic minorities are not randomly distributed throughout the country. Their concentration in particular conurbations means that, at least in statistical terms, they are in a position to influence voting strength in those areas. Within these conurbations, they are even further concentrated in some parliamentary constituencies and local election wards and are therefore in a position to make an impact on the overall voting turnout in those inner-city constituencies and wards. For example, according to the 1981 census, there were 58 constituencies with more than 15 per cent of the total population living in households with head born in the New Commonwealth and Pakistan. Nineteen of them had more than 25 per cent and seven had over 33 per cent (with three approaching almost half: Birmingham Ladywood, Brent South, and Ealing Southall). There are many others with an ethnic minority population of between 10 and

15 per cent. These figures do not take into account ethnic minorities where the head of household was born in this country. However, it is estimated that in 1985 there are about 100 parliamentary constituencies in England with an ethnic minority population of over 10 per cent.

As far as the local election wards are concerned, there are now several hundred with more than 15 per cent ethnic minority population, and several with almost 50 per cent. The highest ethnic minority population of 85.4 per cent was in Northcote ward in the Borough of Ealing, where it was estimated that almost 76 per cent of electors in 1981 were Asians out of a total of 8,148 electors on the register. Glebe ward in the same borough had almost 60 per cent Asian electors. It must be pointed out, however, that counting Asian names on the register is an under-estimation of their actual numbers in the population as some Asians do have anglicized names. There is also under-registration among Asians compared with whites.[2] This means that the real number of eligible Asians and other ethnic minorities to be included in the register will be greater than estimated. Similarly, the total ethnic minority population is always under-estimated because of the lack of the ethnic question in the 1981 census, as referred above.

It is worth stressing again that it is not only the actual number of ethnic minority electors in the same constituencies that makes them 'important' but also their relative concentration in these constituencies that places them in a position to influence the outcome of elections. For example, at the time of the 1979 general election our analysis showed that in some constituencies there were roughly as many ethnic minority electors on the electoral register as there were New Commonwealth and Pakistan origin citizens recorded in the 1971 census. For instance, there were 11,000 Asian names on the register in Leicester South constituency, about 10,000 in Birmingham Sparkbrook, almost 12,000 in Bradford West, and so on. When we looked at the proportion of the total electorate who were ethnic minorities in individual constituencies or wards, the importance of the 'ethnic minority vote' became even clearer (Anwar 1980a: 46). (See *Table 4.*)

Second, the level of political awareness among ethnic minorities has increased over the past two decades. This is partly because they have recognized that their sense of security in this country can be buttressed by such an awareness, and partly because an increasing number of ethnic minority organizations are articulating issues such as race relations and immigration controls which impinge on their sense of security. The ethnic minority press has also played an important role in the creation of

Table 4 *A select list of wards where over half of the population was composed of ethnic minorities, based on 1981 census*

Ward	Borough/district	Percentage population with head of household born in NCWP
Northcote	Ealing	85.4
Soho	Birmingham	71.7
Glebe	Ealing	71.0
University	Bradford	67.6
Brookhouse	Blackburn	66.1
Wycliffe	Leicester	65.7
Spitalsfield	Tower Hamlets	63.1
Spinney Hill	Leicester	61.8
Mount Pleasant	Ealing	58.8
Sparkbrook	Birmingham	55.0
Upton	Newham	55.0
Kennington	Newham	55.0
Handsworth	Birmingham	54.0
Wembley Central	Brent	53.3
Kensal Rise	Brent	52.9
Sparkhill	Birmingham	52.6
Aston	Birmingham	51.0

this awareness. In this regard, they are responding to speeches and comments that are widely disseminated by the mass media including the ethnic minority press, and particularly during election campaigns, and are thus in a position to take such action individually or through the organizations to which they belong to guarantee their own future in this country.

Third, the presence of National Front and other anti-immigrant candidates in elections has increased their awareness of the political issues, and contributed towards an increasing degree of political mobilization and, indeed, participation in elections, in order to counter the anti-immigrant propaganda.

Fourth, and equally important, is the response of the major political parties to the publication of three election studies on this subject. These parties not only felt the need to take steps to involve ethnic minority communities in their activities but also openly sought their vote in various elections between 1974 and the general election in 1983 (Anwar and Kohler 1975; Anwar 1980a, 1984a).

For all these reasons, the phenomenon of the ethnic minority voter participating in an election is no longer a 'flash in the pan' but is likely to become a permanent feature of British political life. The absence of ethnic minority MPs is apparent and perhaps inevitable given our present electoral arrangements. For example, if their true numbers were represented in parliament, there should be 25–30 MPs of ethnic minority origin. There is none at the moment. Any minority group could be influential in a marginal constituency, but the ethnic minority electors are better placed to do this because of their concentrations in certain areas. Some indications of the size of this potential influence were gained in the October 1974, May 1979, and June 1983 general elections (Anwar and Kohler 1975; Anwar 1980a, 1984a). For example, at the time of the 1983 general election it was pointed out that there were 18 parliamentary seats with ethnic minority populations of 5 per cent or more which the Conservatives would notionally have won in 1979 and which were vulnerable to a 5 per cent two-party swing to Labour. There were also 25 such Labour-held seats which would be lost on the same swing to the Conservatives, and a further 10 which Labour would lose if the swing were up to 7.5 per cent. Additionally, there was one seat which the Liberals would notionally have won in 1979 but which they would lose on a 4.6 per cent swing to Labour. Altogether, there were 53 such constituencies (Fitz-Gerald 1983).

The Community Relations Commission's election study in 1974 showed that there were 76 constituencies in February 1974 and 85 in October 1974 in which ethnic minority voters could make a significant impact on the outcome of national elections. To the extent that these constituencies were marginal, the ethnic minority vote could influence the outcome of elections and it did so in October 1974. That study showed that the ethnic minorities played a significant part in determining the general outcome of the election since a substantial majority of ethnic minority voters cast their vote for the Labour party even though they were not inflexibly committed to that particular party. Because of the numbers and concentrations of ethnic minorities, they hold an important strategic position in the areas of their residence, particularly now that in 1985 the two-party system has declined considerably. At the time of the 1951 general election, 96.8 per cent of the British voters voted for Conservative and Labour candidates, but this share was down to 75 per cent in 1974 and 70 per cent in 1983. In the 1980s, we have a new main political party, the Social Democratic Party (SDP). Although the Liberal and Social Democratic parties received a 25.4 per cent share of the vote, they only won 23 seats in the June 1983 general election, whereas the Labour party won 209 seats with 27.6 per cent of the vote. The SDP and Liberal parties are questioning the two-party system and arguing for proportional representation in Britain. They also feel that ethnic minorities would benefit from this change. But the chances of getting the electoral system changed to some sort of proportional system would depend on the Liberals and SDP forming a government or suceeding in making it the price for supporting a minority Conservative or Labour government in a hung parliament. Moreover, the new electoral system would not be a party-list system, but some form of the single transferable vote which will be less helpful to ethnic minorities (Crewe 1983: 280). So the answer for the ethnic minorities at the moment is to get involved in the main political parties as members, become officials, and get elected to parliament and local councils.

The awareness among the main political parties of the importance of ethnic minorities in the areas where they are concentrated has increased in the last decade and they now acknowledge this publicly. For example, in 1982, before the 1983 general election, all four main political parties discussed the importance of the ethnic minority vote at their annual conferences. The Conservative party held a fringe meeting on the subject where at least two Ministers and the Chairman of the Sub-Committee (of the Home Affairs Committee) on Race and Immigration spoke. It was a well attended meeting and the message for the party workers was that they should find ways and means of attracting ethnic minorities to the Conservative party and to get the ethnic minority vote at the next general election. The same sort of discussions took place at the other party conferences. This shows that the political parties would now like to seek the support of ethnic minorities quite publicly rather than treating them as a problem and a subject for debates, as happened in the 1960s and 1970s.

In a speech in July 1984, the then Home Secretary reaffirmed the government's intentions about the participation of ethnic minorities in the full democratic process of the country. He said,

'In a democracy, the most fundamental expression of consultation and involvement is voting in elections, and I want to see the fullest participation of all sections of the community in elections. As institutions adjust to become more open to ethnic minorities, so will prejudice and mistrust between communities be diminished. What we need, therefore, are more black decision takers in all our institutions.'

                                                                (Leon Brittan, 23 July 1984)

He added that in this context, he would like to see much greater participation by ethnic minorities in elections.[3] Now that ethnic minorities are a
permanent part of our society, it is relevant to understand how they see
political issues compared with white people from the same areas; also how
'race relations' generally have been seen by the British people in the last
two decades.

3 Race relations issues in the political context

Before we look at how ethnic minorities and white electors see the specific aspects of race relations, it will be useful to review the attitudes of these two groups to race relations generally. As Lord Scarman stressed when he was carrying out his inquiry into the serious disorders in Brixton on 10 to 12 April 1981: 'The point has often been put to this Inquiry, and I think everybody accepts it, that we are as much concerned with attitudes and beliefs as we are with facts' (*Financial Times*, 15 July 1981). Two surveys undertaken in 1975 and 1981 to find out what ordinary people, both ethnic minorities and whites, think about 'race relations' in Britain are used here to look at the trends in this context. Respondents were asked whether race relations in the country as a whole were getting better, remaining the same, or getting worse.[1]

In the 1975 survey (CRC 1976) 44 per cent of ethnic minority respondents felt that race relations were getting better, as did 32 per cent of whites. On the other hand, only 13 per cent of the ethnic minority and 20 per cent of white respondents throught that race relations were getting worse in the country as a whole. (See *Table 5* for details.) The situation in 1981 was dramatically different from that revealed in the 1975 survey (Anwar 1981b: 14). In the 1981 survey nearly half of the ethnic minority respondents and one third of the whites thought race relations were getting worse and only 18 per cent of ethnic minorities and 25 per cent of whites thought they were getting better. Most noticeable is the change in opinion of ethnic minority people between those years: fewer ethnic minorities than whites thought race relations had improved.

It was interesting to note from the 1981 survey that among the ethnic minority respondents, those born in Britain and those more fluent in English were more likely to think race relations had deteriorated. Among the different ethnic minority groups, the West Indians and the Cypriots

Table 5 *Race relations in the country as a whole*

	Ethnic minorities						Whites	
	All		West Indians		Asians		All	
	1981	1975	1981	1975	1981	1975	1981	1975
	(1,057)	(966)	(370)	(324)	(330)	(584)	(1,073)	(1,050)
	%	%	%	%	%	%	%	%
Better	18	44	17	46	16	43	25	32
Same	28	31	25	26	33	33	35	37
Worse	47	13	52	16	43	11	33	20
Don't know	7	12	6	12	8	12	7	10

were marginally more likely to think race relations had become worse. The Chinese respondents were the most likely to say race relations had improved. However, even within this ethnic group, just as many thought they had deteriorated.

Looking to the future, respondents were also asked in the 1981 survey whether they thought the feelings between whites and ethnic minorities would get better, worse, or stay the same over the next five years. Respondents generally did not display much optimism. Over half (53 per cent) of the ethnic minorities thought race relations would get worse, as did 43 per cent of the whites. Again, among the ethnic minority respondents, it was the young people, those born in Britain, educated, fluent in English, who were most pessimistic about race relations in the future (Anwar 1981b).

Two other findings from the 1981 survey are relevant to the political context: white people's views of ethnic minorities and the overall status of ethnic minorities in British society compared with whites. As far as the views of white respondents were concerned, over three-quarters said that they did not mind them being here, as shown in *Table 6*.

The younger the person, the more likely they were to say 'I have never minded them being here', and those living in areas with smaller numbers of ethnic minorities were also more likely to hold views closer to this statement.

As far as the overall status of the ethnic minorities in British society was concerned, almost 70 per cent of ethnic minorities felt that their status was worse. Eighty-five per cent of Africans and 83 per cent of West Indians considered that ethnic minorities were in a worse position in

Table 6 *Whites' response as to whether or not they minded ethnic minorities being in Britain*

	(1,073) %
I have never minded them being here	67
The more I see of ethnic minority people, the less I mind them being here	10
The more I see of ethnic minority people, the more I mind them being here	11
I have always minded them being here	8
Don't know	3

British society than whites (92 per cent of young West Indians felt this way). (*See Table 7* for details.)

It is significant that 58 per cent of Asians, but also 58 per cent of whites, were inclined to agree with the ethnic minorities' assessment of their position in British society as being 'worse'.

It is clear that the ethnic minorities do feel they are disadvantaged in comparison with the white population. This feeling has implications, particularly for their participation in the political process. However, the

Table 7 *Relative status of ethnic minorities*

	Ethnic minorities			Whites
	All ethnic minorities (1,057) %	West Indians (370) %	Asians (330) %	All (1,073) %
Ethnic minority have better or worse status or position in British society than white people				
Better	2	1	2	4
Worse	69	83	58	58
Same	17	9	20	25
Don't know	12	7	19	13

white population would also now appear to be aware of the disadvantaged position of ethnic minorities and this suggests that politicians need not fear the resentment of the white population over remedial action to improve race relations and provide equal opportunity for everybody in our society. Major initiatives are, therefore, needed to improve the relative position of ethnic minorities and to increase their involvement in the life of our society, including in the political process, improving relations between them and the majority white population.

The opinions of ethnic minorities and white people on the political questions of the day and about which political parties are best equipped to deal with the issues of race relations are important, since these opinions will influence the electors' support for a particular party in elections. Up to the October 1974 general election no special survey was undertaken to obtain some measure of the ethnic minorities' interest in political issues, many of which formed crucial parts of party manifestos. At both the October 1974 and May 1979 general elections special surveys were undertaken to find out how both ethnic minorities and white people rated election issues. They were asked to say whether they thought each issue was 'extremely important', 'quite important', 'not very important', or 'not at all important.' Altogether, 690 and 1,138 respondents were interviewed in 1974 and 1979 respectively.

The 1974 survey showed that, whilst race relations was an extremely important issue to the ethnic minorities, it was not seen in the same way by the white people, as can be seen from *Table 8* (58 per cent Afro-Caribbeans and 56 per cent Asians compared with only 29 per cent whites).

It is clear from the table that whites rated all the issues, except race relations, somewhat higher than the ethnic minorities. The need for more schools was more important to the ethnic minorities, probably because of their younger populations and their awareness of the shortage of schools in the inner-city areas in which they live. In the 1979 survey, generally all the listed issues (see *Table 9*) were thought to be either 'extremely' or 'quite' important to the majority of electors; unemployment, prices, education, law and order, and the health service were seen as the most important issues. These findings were very much in line with the results of opinion polls conducted during the election campaign. Interestingly, 'improving race relations' was ranked in the middle in terms of its importance and therefore was higher in ranking than was the case in 1974 (Anwar 1980a).

Looking at different ethnic groups, it appears from *Table 9* that all respondents rated the two issues of 'keeping prices down' and 'reducing

Table 8 Importance of issues – 1974 Survey

	Total (690)		White (353)		Afro-Caribbean (116)		Asian (219)	
	Extremely important %	Quite important %	Extremely important %	Quite important %	Extremely important %	Quite important %	Extremely important %	Quite important %
Keeping prices down	81	15	88	9	83	14	71	25
Building more houses	69	24	75	20	74	23	58	32
Reducing unemployment	62	28	65	27	61	30	56	29
Protecting people's privacy	57	30	69	24	53	40	40	35
Building more schools	57	29	57	24	60	34	57	34
Protecting freedom of speech	54	29	66	23	45	41	41	33
Improving race relations	42	30	29	28	58	33	56	32
Equal rights for women	38	33	40	32	41	34	33	33

unemployment' as 'extremely' important.[2] However, the ethnic background of respondents influenced their perception of other issues. For
example, education was felt to be of relatively greater importance by Afro-
Caribbean respondents. 'Improving race relations' was rated as the most
important (No. 1) issue by both Afro-Caribbeans and Asians but was rated
twelfth out of 14 by white people. Closer inspection of the data showed
that of the white and Afro-Caribbean respondents, those in the younger
age groups (18 to 34 years) were more likely to see 'improving race
relations' as an important issue than were older people. However, among
the Asian respondents, the level of importance placed on this issue did
not vary with age.

It is interesting to note from *Table 9* that there was a tendency for Afro-
Caribbean responents to attribute a higher level of importance to every
issue than did the Asians. This may be because of their greater
experience of living in Britain compared with Asians. But the general
awareness among ethnic minorities of the wider issues facing the country
is a good sign and shows that they feel a part of the society.

In the 1983 Harris Research Centre survey, 'unemployment' was seen
by 67 per cent Afro-Caribbeans and 71 per cent Asians as one of the 'two
most important election issues'. While 'immigration and nationality' as an
election issue was mentioned only by 17 per cent Afro-Caribbeans and 36
per cent Asians (Harris Research Centre 1983). There are no comparable
figures for whites. We have seen that in the 1979 survey, race relations as
an election issue was rated seventh out of 14 issues by respondents as a
whole but that it was rated as the most important one by the ethnic
minorities. The reason for this is that it usually directly affects ethnic
minorities more than whites.

In this section we look at the reactions of electors and candidates to
specific aspects of race relations as well as their opinions as to which
political parties are best able to deal with these issues. But before we look
at these opinions, it is relevant to quote sections from the national
manifestos of the three main political parties in 1979 concerning policies
that directly affect ethnic minorities.

The Conservative party manifesto stated:

'The rights of all British citizens legally settled here are equal before
the law whatever their race, colour or creed. And their opportunities
ought to be equal too. The ethnic minorities have already made a
valuable contribution to the life of our nation. But firm immigration
control for the future is essential if we are to achieve good community

Table 9 *Rating of issues by different ethnic groups – 1979 survey*

	Total		White		Afro-Caribbean		Asian	
	Mean score	%	Mean score	%	Mean score	%	Mean score	%
(1) Keeping prices down	3.69	95	3.71 (1)	96	3.75 (2)	96	3.63 (2)	95
(2) Reducing unemployment	3.65	94	3.67 (2)	95	3.71 (4)	95	3.61 (3)	91
(3) Providing better education	3.58	91	3.53 (5)	92	3.74 (3)	98	3.59 (4)	90
(4) Tighter controls to keep law and order	3.58	87	3.63 (3)	91	3.60 (6)	90	3.49 (5)	82
(5) Improving the Health Service	3.56	91	3.60 (4)	92	3.64 (5)	93	3.48 (6)	90
(6) Lowering of taxation	3.44	86	3.41 (9)	87	3.53 (7)	89	3.44 (7)	83
(7) Improving race relations	3.40	82	3.15 (12)	74	3.75 (1)	93	3.65 (1)	91
(8) Protecting people's privacy	3.37	83	3.49 (6)	90	3.34 (9)	84	3.16 (10)	71
(9) Building more houses	3.34	82	3.36 (10)	85	3.50 (8)	88	3.26 (9)	76
(10) Getting a better deal for Britain in the Common Market	3.28	69	3.42 (8)	82	3.07 (12)	61	3.06 (11)	55
(11) Controlling the Trade Union's power	3.28	72	3.45 (7)	85	3.06 (13)	68	3.02 (13)	55
(12) Protecting freedom of speech	3.23	76	3.34 (11)	86	3.23 (11)	80	3.04 (12)	62
(13) Lowering mortgage rates	3.16	75	3.05 (13)	71	3.30 (10)	82	3.27 (8)	79
(14) Equal rights for women	2.94	65	2.97 (14)	69	3.05 (14)	64	2.87 (14)	61

Figures in brackets show ranking position.

Percentages show those people answering 'extremely important' or 'quite important' to each issue.

Source: Anwar, 1980a.

relations. It will end persistent fears about levels of immigration and will remove from those settled, and in many cases born here, the label of "immigrant".

(i) We shall introduce a new British Nationality Act to define entitlement to British citizenship and to the right of abode in this country. It will not adversely affect the right of anyone now permanently settled here.

(ii) We shall end the practice of allowing permanent settlement for those who come here for a temporary stay.

(iii) We shall limit entry of parents, grandparents and children over 18 to a small number of urgent compassionate cases.

(iv) We shall end the concession introduced by the Labour government in 1974 to husbands and male fiances.

(v) We shall severely restrict the issue of work permits.

(vi) We shall introduce a Register of those Commonwealth wives and children entitled to entry for settlement under the 1971 Immigration Act.

(vii) We shall then introduce a quota system, covering everyone outside the European Community, to control all entry for settlement.

(viii) We shall take firm action against illegal immigrants and overstayers and help those immigrants who genuinely wish to leave this country – but there can be no question of compulsory repatriation.

We will encourage the improvement of language training in schools and factories and of training facilities for the young unemployed in the ethnic communities. But these measures will achieve little without the effective control of immigration. That is essential for racial harmony in Britain today.'

(Conservative party 1979: 20–21)

The Labour party's 1979 manifesto had this to say on race relations and other related issues:

'Labour has already strengthened the legislation protecting minorities. The next Labour government will continue to protect the community against discrimination and racialism. We will:

– give a strong lead by promoting equality of opportunity at work throughout the public sector;

– help those whose first language is not English;

- monitor all government and local authority services to ensure that minorities are receiving fair treatment;
- consider what measures may be necessary to clarify the role of the Public Order Act and to strengthen and widen the scope of the Race Relations Act;
- review the 1824 Vagrancy Act, with a view to the repeal of Section 4.

Large-scale migration to this country is ending, but we will have some major commitments to fulfil. Labour will honour these. A quota would merely cause even longer delays for dependants. Our whole immigration and citizenship law needs revision. Progress has already been made on this with the publication of a Government Green Paper.'

(Labour party 1979: 29)

The Liberal party manifesto was more detailed and dealt with nationality and immigration matters as well as minority rights, viz:

'There should be only one class of citizenship for citizens of the UK and colonies. We would abolish the discrimination against non-patrials which creates second-class citizens. Citizens of the UK and colonies, including residents of Commonwealth countries who accepted the offer of remaining UK citizens when independence was granted, should have a right of entry. Spouses, children and other dependants of UK residents should be allowed to join their families in Britain and all children who have been born abroad of British mothers must have automatic rights of citizenship. Liberals deplore the Tory policy of inflaming people's fears about unrestricted immigration when the numbers of immigrants are actually falling. We should, wherever practicable, accept *bona fide* refugees.'

On minority rights, it stated that:

'Britain is a diverse and multicultural society and Liberals rejoice in its richness, which owes much to the peoples of many different ethnic origins and cultures who have chosen to live here. We defend their right to maintain and develop their own traditions. Minority groups must be allowed to practise and advocate their beliefs, provided this does not reduce the freedom of others. We will protect and defend the rights of minorities by:
- a comprehensive law outlawing discrimination on grounds of race, sex or political belief with enforcement through a single Anti-Discrimination Board;

- providing a legal right for nomadic people to live according to their life-style so long as this does not harm others;
- removing all legal discriminations based on sexual orientation.'

(Liberal party 1979: 8–9)

However, in spite of these declarations, race relations was not seen as a major election issue in the 1979 general election by the three political parties. How did the electors and the candidates see some of these issues?

First, let us look at the opinions of candidates. We found that Labour and Liberal party candidates attributed a similar degree of importance to race relations as an election issue (49 per cent for the Liberals and 47 per cent for Labour). Conservatives, on the other hand, were inclined to see this issue as relatively less important (43 per cent). In addition, there was a noticeable difference of opinion between the Conservative candidates who were later elected and those who were not. Those who were not elected were more likely to consider the issue to be more important (45 per cent) than those who were elected (36 per cent). As could be expected, National Front candidates considered the improvement of race relations to be 'not very important' (19 per cent).

In view of racial problems which had occurred in some areas, and in particular the increased racial tension resulting from demonstrations and counter-demonstrations by National Front supporters and their opponents which took place a few weeks before the election, it is surprising that greater importance was not placed on this issue. Weighed against this is the fact that many of the candidates who participated in the survey were unlikely to be standing in constituencies with a high proportion of ethnic minorities; therefore, race relations was unlikely to be a major issue of concern to their voters. Nevertheless, it is worth stressing that those Conservatives who got elected tended to attribute lower degrees of importance to the issue of improving race relations than did their colleagues who were not elected. One of the reasons for this attitude could be that a large number of those Conservatives who were elected were more likely not to have ethnic minority populations in their areas.

In order to ascertain candidates' opinions on specific issues concerning race relations, they were asked to indicate the issues that they considered to be particularly important at a *national level*. Their responses showed a general concern with improving opportunities for ethnic minorities in education, employment, and housing. In this regard, suggestions were made for improving educational facilities (e.g. the teaching of English and the introduction of special educational projects), enforcing equality of opportunity in employment, and the withdrawal of the use of public facilities from racialist groups such as the National Front. More Labour candidates were in favour of denying public facilities to racialist groups (20 per cent) than were either Liberal (6 per cent) or Conservative (1 per cent) candidates.

In order to probe further the views of candidates on issues which directly affect ethnic minority groups, they were asked for their opinion on the statements mentioned in *Table 10*.

The results in the table show that there was not much difference of opinion between candidates of the three political parties in supporting the principle of equality and there was virtually no support for a policy of compulsory repatriation. However, 20 per cent of the Conservative candidates were in favour of voluntary repatriation (to encourage ethnic minority groups and their children born in the UK to return to their native countries) compared with 2 per cent each of the Labour and the Liberal candidates. In another survey at the time of the 1983 general election, 19 per cent of Conservatives still supported voluntary repatriation and virtually all Labour and Alliance candidates opposed this (Anwar 1984a: 24). Once again, in this survey there was almost universal

Table 10 *Candidates' reactions to certain issues*

	Total (573) %	Con. (219) %	Lab. (107) %	Lib. (216) %
To make ethnic minority groups return to their native countries				
Support	2	1	—	2
Oppose	95	92	100	97
To draw up a register				
Support	43	84	7	22
Oppose	43	6	79	61
To treat all people equally				
Support	95	92	98	99
Oppose	1	2	2	—
To encourage ethnic minority groups including children born in the UK to return to their native country				
Support	9	20	2	2
Oppose	76	54	97	88

support among candidates of all four main political parties for two issues: treating ethnic minorities the same as white people and encouraging ethnic minority groups to participate in the activities of the community as a whole (97 per cent and 96 per cent respectively). Furthermore, apart from some of the Conservatives, the candidates from the three other parties in 1983 claimed to be almost universally in favour of positive action. The Conservative candidates were rather more divided on the issue of positive action and slightly more (42 per cent) candidates supported than opposed (38 per cent) positive action.

Looking at the 1979 survey of candidates, a major difference emerged with regard to the drawing up of a register for dependants (see *Table 10*). The majority of Conservatives supported this proposal (as it was in the party's manifesto) while the majority of both Labour and Liberal party candidates were opposed to it.

As politicians, when elected, are responsible for making more relevant policies about any issues facing the country, we decided to find out how they viewed the race relations situation. Therefore, the candidates were asked in 1979 and 1983 whether they felt that the relationships between ethnic minorities and the indigenous white community were getting better, getting worse, or remaining the same in the country as a whole. The 1979 survey showed that only 19 per cent of candidates thought that things were getting worse. As might be expected, the Labour candidates were more likely than other party candidates to think the situation was improving because they belonged to the party in power which was responsible for race relations policies before the 1979 general election. We present results of the 1979 and 1983 surveys in *Table 11*.

Table 11 *Race relations as seen by candidates in the country as a whole*

	Total		Conservative		Labour		Liberal		SDP*
	1979	1983	1979	1983	1979	1983	1979	1983	1983
	(573)	(662)	(219)	(185)	(107)	(190)	(216)	(133)	(129)
	%	%	%	%	%	%	%	%	%
Getting better	26	21	16	27	43	19	29	23	16
Remaining the same	35	37	40	50	31	26	34	34	36
Getting worse	19	33	20	16	14	46	19	36	38
DK/NA/Unsure†	20	9	24	8	12	8	18	8	11

* SDP was formed in 1981.

† DK = Don't know, NA = No answer.

Clearly, in 1983 opinion was divided amongst those who thought that race relations in the country as a whole were getting worse (33 per cent), remaining the same (37 per cent) and getting better (21 per cent). Like the Labour candidates in the 1979 survey, the Conservative candidates in the 1983 survey (then the party in power) were more optimistic than other candidates: 27 per cent thought feelings were getting better compared with 19 per cent of Labour, 23 per cent of Liberal, and only 16 per cent of SDP candidates. On the other hand 46 per cent Labour compared with only 16 per cent Conservative candidates said that race relations were getting worse in the country as a whole (for details see *Table 11*).

In the 1979 survey, candidates were asked for their views on race relations policies and how they could be improved. Only 22 per cent felt the policies were good or satisfactory; the majority (63 per cent) felt that they were unsatisfactory for various reasons; 10 per cent felt that race relations policies were not strictly enforced and unlikely to be effective in the absence of changes in attitudes on the part of the white population to ethnic minority groups. Labour and Liberal candidates were more likely to feel that these policies were good or satisfactory compared to Conservatives (36 per cent, 31 per cent, and 18 per cent respectively). Other responses were unspecific and, in any event, involved too few candidates for meaningful conclusions to be drawn. What improvements or changes in these policies did they envisage?

Against the background of the view by some politicians that a curb on immigration will improve race relations, it is interesting that only 4 per cent felt that a complete curb on immigration was likely to achieve such an improvement; a further 6 per cent felt that a policy of compulsory repatriation was likely to do so. The majority felt that it was the provision of better educational facilities for ethnic minority groups in this country that was likely to improve race relations. How do these views compare with those of the electors?

In other to explore the electors' knowledge of the policies of various political parties, we asked them to identify the political parties which supported the following proposals in their manifestos in 1979:

- compulsory repatriation;
- introduction of a register of dependants;
- equal treatment for ethnic minorities;
- voluntary repatriation.

Three-quarters of the Afro-Caribbean and half the Asian respondents associated the policy of compulsory repatriation with the National Front party. But a significant proportion (22 per cent) of respondents also associated 'compulsory repatriation' with the Conservative party. Only 2 per cent associated this policy with the Labour party. In this regard, there were a few differences between different ethnic groups, with 27 per cent of Afro-Caribbeans, 23 per cent of Asians, and 21 per cent of white people associating this policy with the Conservative party.

Over a third (36 per cent) of the respondents associated the drawing up of an eligibility register with the Conservative party. More ethnic minority respondents did so (Afro-Caribbeans 44 per cent, Asians 38 per cent) than white people (34 per cent). Nevertheless, there were still many people who thought that this policy was part of the Labour party's manifesto. Twenty-one per cent of white people and 17 per cent of both Afro-Caribbeans and Asians identified it with the Labour party. In fact, as can be seen from the results of the candidates' survey mentioned above, only 7 per cent of Labour candidates supported this proposal compared with 84 per cent of Conservative and 22 per cent of Liberal candidates.

The majority (62 per cent) of respondents saw Labour as the party advocating equal treatment for ethnic minorities in this country. This was even higher – more than two-thirds – among the ethnic minority population. Only 18 per cent considered this to be a Conservative party policy and even fewer (9 per cent) considered it to be a Liberal one.

Over a third of the respondents (35 per cent) identified voluntary repatriation with the National Front although over a quarter (27 per cent) believed that it was also a Conservative party policy. There was little difference of opinion between people of different ethnic groups. Only 4 per cent of respondents thought the Labour party was in favour of this and 1 per cent believed that it was also a Liberal party policy. This corresponds with the candidates' survey results mentioned above which showed that 20 per cent of Conservative candidates, but only 2 per cent of Labour candidates, favoured voluntary repatriation.

Respondents were then asked to indicate the political party which they felt was most capable of providing:

– equal employment opportunities for ethnic minority groups;
– better housing conditions for these groups;
– better educational facilities to deal with their specific needs;
– equal treatment generally for ethnic minority groups.

As the following table shows, in each instance the Labour party was rated better than the Conservative party among all groups of respondents.

Table 12 *Party most sympathetic to these issues*

	Total (1,138) %	White (582) %	Afro-Caribbean (144) %	Asian (397) %
Equal employment opportunities				
Labour	59	53	67	65
Conservative	7	10	2	5
Better housing conditions				
Labour	56	53	63	60
Conservative	26	26	27	26
Better educational facilities				
Labour	57	52	63	62
Conservative	9	12	4	7
Equal treatment generally				
Labour	60	55	69	65
Conservative	24	25	20	23

Totals do not add up to 100 per cent because some respondents mentioned other parties while others were 'undecided' and did not express their opinions.

A similar Labour advantage was found in the 1974 survey (Anwar and Kohler 1975). Labour was seen then to be most sympathetic to these particular issues by respondents from all ethnic backgrounds. In order to explore the reasons for this advantage, in 1974 and 1979 respondents were asked to outline some action which the Labour party had taken which was of direct benefit to ethnic minority groups.

A third of the respondents could not think of anything which the Labour government had done to benefit minority groups and 13 per cent were certain that they had done nothing. Other respondents replied as follows:

'Passed the Race Relations Act of 1976' (17 per cent);
'Allowed dependants to enter the country' (16 per cent);
'Allowed fiancés to marry Asian girls here' (16 per cent);
'United families' (11 per cent)

Slightly more Afro-Caribbeans (19 per cent) mentioned the passing of the Race Relations Act 1976 than did Asians (15 per cent); understandably, Asians were more concerned with allowing dependants and fiancés to enter this country than Afro-Caribbeans because of their late migration and cultural and marriage patterns.

These responses pointed to a greater level of awareness among respondents about action taken by government in the field of immigration and race relations when compared with the 1974 results. In 1974 many more respondents (70 per cent) were unable to think of anything which the Labour government had done which had been of direct benefit to ethnic minorities. The only major issue raised then was that of the amnesty which was granted to illegal immigrants shortly before the 1974 survey. Twelve per cent of respondents mentioned this in 1974 compared with 6 per cent in 1979.

In the 1979 survey we also asked electors whether they felt that the relationships between white people and ethnic minorities were getting better, getting worse, or remaining the same in the country as a whole. More than 32 per cent saw the situation getting worse. White people were least optimistic, with 37 per cent seeing the situation as getting worse compared with 29 per cent of Afro-Caribbeans and 27 per cent of Asians. Only 18 per cent of white respondents thought the situation had improved compared with 36 per cent Afro-Caribbeans and 25 per cent Asians. When we compare these findings with the 1981 survey referred to, we find that in 1981 people of all ethnic groups were less optimistic about race relations (see *Table 5*).

Electors were also asked their opinions of governments' race relations policies prior to the 1979 general election. One in three electors thought that race relations policies were adequate and some thought they could be better. Criticisms were made by some saying that government had failed to stop discrimination in employment and other fields. One Afro-Caribbean respondent commented, 'I think race relations policy is bad. The parties play politics with it. I don't want ethnic people to be treated different – just the same as everyone else.' A young Asian reacted strongly to race relations policies before 1979 by saying, 'It's a whitewash. It's just on paper. In practice it's a failure.' Another Asian reacted, 'I feel that there are double standards about this. Despite the Race Relations Act, there is still ill-feeling between white and non-white people.' One Asian thought that race relations policies were ineffective: 'I don't think it is effective because it needs to have more power to act'. Similar sorts of comments were made about the ineffectiveness of the race relations policies of government at the time of our research on the 1983 general election.

The majority of people in our surveys thought that the Labour party was encouraging equality between different racial groups although this was also outlined in the Conservative and the Liberal parties' (also SDP in

1983) manifestos in 1979 and 1983. For example, the Conservative party manifesto for the 1983 general election included:

> *'Immigration; firm and fair.* We are utterly opposed to racial discrimination wherever it occurs, and we are determined to see that there is real equality of opportunity. The Conservative party is, and always has been, strongly opposed to unfairness, harassment and persecution, whether it be inspired by racial, religious or ideological motives.
>
> 'To have good community relations, we have to maintain effective immigration control. Since 1979, immigration for settlement has dropped sharply to the lowest level since control of immigration from the Commonwealth began more than twenty years ago. By passing the British Nationality Act, we have created a secure system of rights and a sound basis for control in the future; and will continue to pursue policies which are strict but fair.'
>
> (Conservative party 1983)

The Labour party's manifesto, *The New Hope For Britain,* for the 1983 general election sets out particular details about equal rights and nationality and immigration:

> *'Equal Rights*
> The next Labour government will lead a political offensive against racial disadvantage, discrimination and harassment; and we have set out our proposals in *Labour's Programme 1982.* To encourage equality and reduce discrimination, we will greatly expand funding to ethnic minority projects. We will also encourage local authorities, in selecting projects under the Urban Programme, to provide for greater ethnic minority participation. We will also:
> - Stimulate a wide range of positive action programmes to ensure that ethnic minorities receive a fair deal – in employment, education, housing and social services; and encourage the keeping of ethnic records, in order to assess the needs of ethnic minorities and take steps to meet them.
> - Launch a major public education initiative aimed at eliminating prejudice.
> - Strengthen the existing Race Relations Act – in particular, to enable us to deal more effectively with racialist literature, speeches and marches; and to remove the exception for seamen recruited abroad.
> - Appoint a senior minister to lead the offensive against racial inequality.

We are concerned that homosexuals are unfairly treated. We will take steps to ensure that they are not unfairly discriminated against – especially in employment and in the definition of privacy contained in the 1967 Act – along the lines set out in Labour's Programme, 1982.

Nationality And Immigration

Through their immigration and nationality laws, the Tories have divided families and caused immense suffering in the immigrant communities. We accept the need for immigration controls. But we will repeal the 1971 Immigration Act and the 1981 British Nationality Act and replace them with a citizenship law that does not discriminate against either women or black and Asian Britons.

Under our *Nationality Act*, we will restore rights removed by the Tories, such as the right to automatic citizenship if born in Britain. The Act will enable other Commonwealth and foreign nationals to acquire citizenship if they qualify by objective tests, and provide a right of appeal against the refusal of an application for citizenship. We will also ensure that the cost of acquiring citizenship will no longer be an obstacle to those who wish to apply.

Under our new *Immigration Act* we will liberalise the age limit criteria for children and the criteria for elderly parents and other relatives. We will simplify the procedures and commit the resources necessary for all applications to be processed promptly; and allow medical examinations, including x-rays, only for medical, not administrative purposes. The race and sex discrimination in the husbands' and fiancés' rules will be ended; we will restore the entitlement to admission to join a woman settled here irrespective of her citizenship, birthplace or ancestry. We will also ensure that immigration officials fully respect the human rights of those seeking entry. We will also:

– Consult Commonwealth governments so as to resolve the question of the other British nationals from independent countries who possess no other citizenship.
– Provide a right of appeal for those who the Home Secretary proposes to deport or exclude on security grounds.
– Establish a more independent and balanced panel of adjudicators for immigration appeals.'

(Labour party 1983)

The Liberal party stand on both nationality and race relations was included in *The Liberal Programme*, endorsed by its Council in July 1982:

'Many groups in our society are oppressed. All have a right to be

respected and represented. To aid this process, there should be a
single Anti-Discrimination Board to combat discrimination on grounds
of race, sex, sexual orientation or religious belief and to help educate
public opinion to understand the rights and values of those who follow
different life styles from the majority. . . . Educational provision for
ethnic minorities should aim to enable these citizens to obtain employment, promotion and training opportunities on an equal basis. Public
authority employers and nationalised industries should be required to
give a positive lead in providing employment and promotion opportunities to citizens from ethnic minority communities.'

(Liberal party 1982)

The SDP's document of September 1982 *Citizen's Rights*, devoted a
chapter to 'Equality of opportunity and minority rights' and stated its
objective, 'to create an open, classless and more equal society which
rejects prejudices based upon sex, race or religion' (SDP 1982).

Some of these commitments by the Liberal and SDP parties were
reflected in the Alliance's manifesto, *Working Together For Britain*, for
the 1983 general election:

'*A new Bill of Rights*. It is shaming that our citizens have so frequently
had to go to the European Court to have basic rights enforced. We
shall incorporate the rights and freedoms of the European Convention
of Human Rights into English, Scottish and Northern Ireland law by
means of a new Bill of Rights Act which will be paramount over all
inconsistent statutes and common law;

We shall create a UK Commission of Human Rights to help people
bring proceedings under the Bill of Rights to secure compliance with
its provisions. This will incorporate the existing Equal Opportunities
Commission and Commission for Racial Equality and will deal with
discrimination on grounds of sex or race;

The Alliance believes that sex and race equality are fundamental to
our society. They will be promoted by positive action in relation e.g. to
public employment policies which will be monitored in central and
local government. Anti-discrimination legislation will be actively
enforced;

Nationality and immigration: we believe the British Nationality Act
1981 to be offensive and discriminatory. We will revert to the simple
concept that all those born in Britain are entitled to British citizenship. There should be objective tests for citizenship and a right of
appeal against refusal. Immigration control will be applied without

discrimination on grounds of sex, race or colour, and rules on dependants will be revised to promote family unity.'

(The Liberal/SDP Alliance 1983)

If we compare the statements made in the three manifestos, the overall objective of all the parties seems to be that there should be equality in society.

It also appears from these manifestos that race relations were a 'valence' issue and not a 'position' issue in the 1979 and 1983 general elections, which means that they were a competence issue rather than an ideological one (Stokes 1966: 170–74).[3] In spite of the above mentioned objectives of the other political parties, generally speaking the information from the 1974 and 1979 surveys referred to above and any evidence we collected at the 1983 general election show that ethnic minorities were relatively satisfied with the Labour race relations policies. The Labour party was seen to be relatively more sympathetic to various problems, especially those relating to ethnic minorities. For example, in the 1974 survey half of the ethnic minority respondents felt that the Labour party was more sympathetic to Asians and West Indians compared with less than 10 per cent each for the Conservatives and the Liberals. This was also pointed out by some ethnic minority papers and by some ethnic minority organizations during the election campaigns. Therefore, it is against this background that we will look later at the voting patterns of ethnic minorities and whites in various elections, living in the same areas.

Before we look at the actual participation of ethnic minorities and others in various elections, it is worth pointing out that on the whole the electors we interviewed were more likely than the candidates to think that feelings between whites and ethnic minorities were getting worse. This finding indicates that electors would like to see more action to improve this situation. Therefore, their expression of party support at elections is probably linked to the policies and image of a particular party.

4 Registration and turnout by ethnic groups

The question of whether ethnic minorities are participating in the political process and are influencing the outcome of elections in Britain depends on several factors. These include whether they register on the Electoral Register; if they are on the register, whether they come out to vote; and how they compare with white people in this respect.

Registration

Registration on the Electoral Register is a fundamental prerequisite for participation in British local, general, and European Assembly elections. To what extent do ethnic minority people register to vote? We look at records of this phenomenon since 1964.

It must be remembered that even where eligible votes are registered, the Electoral Register tends to provide an incomplete measure of all those who are eligible because it is usually published some four months after it is compiled and is invariably 16 months out of date when it is replaced. Thus 'at all times, large numbers of dead people are on the register while people who have moved are not registered in respect of their current addresses' (Leonard 1968: 16). Not surprisingly, therefore, one study of the level of accuracy of the Electoral Register found that it is at any time no more than 94 per cent accurate as a record of all those who are eligible to vote. It tends to become inaccurate at a rate of a half per cent per month due to removals, right up to the last month before it is replaced, when its accuracy drops to 87 per cent (Gray and Gee 1967).

Nevertheless, these problems apart, ethnic minority groups experience difficulties in registering as electors. Some have language difficulties; others may not be familiar with their rights; still others probably feel their stay in Britain is a temporary one and do not therefore feel impelled to involve themselves in the political process. One study in 1964 showed that less than half of all Commonwealth immigrants were registered (Deakin 1965). The proportion of ethnic minorities on the register increased in 1966, but nevertheless, a sample survey of 227 Asians and Afro-Caribbeans and 175 whites in 1974 showed that ethnic minorities were five times as likely not to have registered to vote as were whites in the same area (Anwar and Kohler 1975). Only 6 per cent of the whites were not registered compared with almost a quarter (24 per cent) of ethnic minorities. The incidence of 'movers in' was also higher among ethnic minorities (19 per cent) compared with whites (14 per cent). When those who had recently moved and new voters (18 years old) were excluded, it was found that only 6 per cent of whites, compared with 27 per cent of Asians and 37 per cent of Afro-Caribbean people, were not registered.

This high level of non-registration was alarming and several organizations – the then Community Relations Commission, community relations councils, political parties, and some ethnic minority organizations – tried to encourage ethnic minority people to register as voters. In 1976 checks in two areas where fieldwork had been undertaken in 1974 showed a great improvement in the level of registration of ethnic minorities. In Birmingham it was found that 5 per cent of Asians and 13 per cent of West Indians were not on the register, compared with 4 per cent of whites. In Bradford, 9 per cent of Asians were not registered as against 5 per cent of whites from the same area (Anwar 1979a). This improvement was partly due to a special campaign launched by the Bradford City Council in 1976 to encourage ethnic minorities and others to register. However, the results from Bradford and Birmingham could not be generalized over the whole country, and we continued our research into this important and fundamental aspect of political participation.

In 1979, we undertook a survey of 24 constituencies spread throughout the country. Fieldwork for this survey was conducted in the three weeks following the general election. The criterion for selecting respondents was as follows: if a person had lived at an address for eight months or less and was not on the register, he or she was classified as a 'recent mover'. If just 18 and not on the register he or she was classified as a 'new voter'; persons who could not be traced in the register were classified as 'not registered'. Information was collected from a total of 823 households comprising 1,927 people. Of these 1,115 were white, 152 Afro-Caribbean, 595 Asian, and 65 were other ethnic groups (e.g. Chinese, Cypriots, and Malaysian).

If we exclude those who were classified as 'new voters' and 'recent movers' we find that 23 per cent of ethnic minority respondents were not registered, whereas for white respondents the percentage of those not on the Electoral Register remains 7 per cent (see *Table 13* below). In other words, the lower tendency to register among ethnic minority groups is not accounted for by a preponderance of 'new voters' and 'recent movers'.

Within the ethnic minority groups, Chinese and Cypriots were slightly less likely to be registered and Afro-Caribbeans were more likely to be registered.

It is interesting to compare these findings with those from the earlier registration survey (carried out in 1974). This comparison shows that the level of registration among all ethnic groups improved slightly (7 per cent) but some ethnic groups improved more than others. For instance, the level of registration among Afro-Caribbeans rose by 18 per cent (from 63 per cent in 1974 to 81 per cent in 1979) while among Asians it increased only marginally from 73 per cent in 1974 to 77 per cent. Among the white population it remained virtually constant (94 per cent in 1974 and 93 per cent in 1979).

It is also interesting to examine the pattern of non-registration in different areas of the country. The results showed wide variation from area to area among ethnic groups. Part of such variation is undoubtedly linked with the policies of local electoral registration offices and with the interest taken by political parties or voluntary groups in persuading various groups to participate in the political process. We found that areas with high levels of non-registration among ethnic minorities included the constituencies of Glasgow Central, Leicester South, Ealing Acton, Bradford West, Coventry North-East, Birmingham Sparkbrook, and Wandsworth-Battersea South. Almost 100 per cent registration was

Table 13 *Registration by Race (excluding new voters and recent movers) in 1979*

	White (1,041)		Afro-Caribbean (145)		Asian (570)		Others (59)		Total ethnic minorities (774)	
	No.	%	No.	%	No.	%	No.	%	No.	%
Registered	964	93	118	81	438	77	43	73	599	77
Not registered	77	7	27	19	132	23	16	27	175	23

recorded in Manchester Ardwick, Preston North, and Wolverhampton South-West. However, data relating to individual constituencies should be regarded merely as indications, since base figures in some of them were small and the fieldwork was undertaken in certain wards.

It is also acknowledged by researchers that residents in inner-city areas have been becoming more mobile, and hence may not be residents at the same address when the Electoral Register is completed. The two surveys in 1974 and 1979 referred to above were conducted mainly in inner-city areas and this is probably one explanation for the high level of non-registration among both whites and ethnic minorities (Anwar and Kohler 1975; Anwar 1980a). To test this, we looked at one OPCS study undertaken in 1981 at the time of the census which confirmed this trend towards a higher proportion of non-registration in inner-city areas, especially in London (Todd and Butcher 1982). This applied to both whites and ethnic minorities. For example, the study showed that in Inner London both the Afro-Caribbeans and Asian people had about double the non-registration rate of white people (24 per cent and 27 per cent as opposed to 12 per cent). Generally the situation with regard to registration had deteriorated in comparison with the Survey of Electoral Registration in 1966 of eligible people in England and Wales (from 3.5 to 4 per cent not registered in 1966, to 6.7 per cent in 1981).

At the time of the GLC election in May 1981, we undertook a survey of registration in three constituencies in London Paddington, Hounslow, and Walthamstow. We covered only one polling district in each constituency, so it is not possible to generalize about the constituencies as a whole. It was discovered, like the previous surveys, that the extent of registration varied between the different ethnic groups. Of those who were eligible to vote, the survey showed that 9 per cent whites, 42 per cent Afro-Caribbeans, and 4 per cent Asians were not on the register. The situation in Paddington was worse, with 17 per cent of all those qualified found to be not on the register, compared with 3 per cent for Hounslow and 4 per cent for Walthamstow.

To continue monitoring progress in the same areas as in 1979, the CRE undertook another survey of registration in 1983. This survey showed that among those qualified to be registered, 17 per cent of whites and 20 per cent of ethnic minorities were not registered (Anwar 1984a). Compared with 1979, the level of registration had fallen amongst white electors from 93 per cent to 81 per cent, which is a surprising finding. But the level of registration for ethnic minorities had improved slightly from 77 per cent to 78 per cent when taken as a group. However, among

Asians, excluding those who were ineligible for inclusion in the register, between 1979 and 1983 the level of registration had increased slightly from 77 per cent to 79 per cent. But the level of registration among Afro-Caribbeans had fallen in 1983 from 81 per cent, the high level recorded in 1979, to 76 per cent. Details of the three surveys referred to above (1974, 1979, and 1983) are given in *Table 14*.

As far as the 'other ethnic minority' category in the table is concerned, the base numbers were too small to draw any firm conclusions, but the indications were that there had been an increase in the level of registration among the groups as the figures in the table suggest.

When we looked at the 1983 survey results at constituency level, it showed that there was quite a lot of variation in registration levels as far as ethnic minorities were concerned. For example, particularly low levels of registration (60 per cent or less) were recorded among ethnic minorities in Ealing Southall, Croydon North-East, Hackney North and Stoke Newington, Norwood, and Walsall South constituencies (Anwar 1984a). On the other hand, Wolverhampton South-West, Preston, Rochdale, Sheffield Heeley, Leicester South, Manchester Gorton, Birmingham Sparkbrook, and Battersea constituencies had over 80 per cent registration among ethnic minorities.

Although steady improvement has taken place in ethnic minority registration levels over the last two decades, and certainly in the last 10 years, the high level of non-registration amongst ethnic minorities, and also now among whites in the inner cities, is alarming and needs action. As the evidence presented above shows, if no action is taken almost one-fifth of ethnic minorities are not in a position to exercise their right to vote.[1] It was in this context that the then Home Secretary, Leon Brittan, said:

> 'I would like to see much greater participation by black people in elections. To vote you must first be registered on the electoral roll. But it is estimated that about 30 per cent of the black community is not so registered, whereas the figure for white non-registration is only 6 per cent. As Home Secretary, I shall see that effective steps are taken to explain the electoral system in clear terms and to improve the completeness and accuracy of the electoral roll.'
>
> (Leon Brittan, 23 July 1984)

To implement this commitment from the government by the Home Secretary, the Home Office decided to arrange several consultative meetings across the country during 1985. The ethnic minority groups, the local Community Relations Councils, the Electoral Registration Officers (EROs),

Table 14 Registration by racial groups: comparison of recent General Elections

	White			Total ethnic minority			Afro-Caribbean			Asian			Other ethnic minority		
	1983 (994) %	1979 (1,041) %	1974 (150) %	1983 (1,020) %	1979 (774) %	1974 (183) %	1983 (152) %	1979 (145) %	1974 (41) %	1983 (822) %	1979 (570) %	1974 (142) %	1983 (46) %	1979 (59) %	1974 —
Registered	81	93	94	78	77	70	76	81	63	79	77	73	78	73	—
Not registered	19	7	6	22	23	30	24	19	27	21	23	27	22	27	—

Note: Percentages are based on those eligible to vote.

and representatives of the CRE and the OPCS were to be present at these meetings to discuss policies and practices in this regard, with a view to improving electoral registration among ethnic minorities. The first such meeting, which covered the Midlands and South Wales, took place in Birmingham on 25 January 1985, hosted by the city council.[2]

Reasons for non-registration include the newness, the language difficulty that Asians and some other ethnic groups face, the general alienation of some groups, and feared harassment and racial attacks from the National Front and other such organizations, who could identify Asians from their names on the register. There is also the fear of 'fishing expeditions' by immigration authorities. Finally, it could be the administrative inefficiency of the Registration offices. However, we need proper research to find out the precise reasons for non-registration among different groups.[3]

Steps are being taken to improve the high level of non-registration among ethnic minorities. Several areas now use either special leaflets designed for ethnic minorities in several languages which go with Form A or a translation of Form A into different languages. Some registration offices – Ealing, for example – now employ full-time, year-round fieldworkers who visit homes from which no Form A has been received during the previous year. Among others, Lambeth and Haringey in London, Birmingham, and Bradford have made special efforts. Hackney in London started a special registration campaign funded by the Greater London Council's Campaign Against Racism. The Home Office has issued a Code of Practice for EROs, which is also relevant in this context. The ethnic minority press has been used and ethnic programmes on radio and television have also helped to make people aware of the importance and the timing of registration. Political parties in some local areas, some ethnic minority organizations, and some local Community Relations Councils have also put in special efforts to increase registration among ethnic minorities.

It is due to such efforts, and an increasing awareness among ethnic minorities of the political process, that their registration level is edging nearer that of white people. But do those who register come out to vote at elections?

Turnout

The analysis of the rates of turnout by different ethnic groups is complicated by the fact that Afro-Caribbeans and other ethnic minorities who have anglicized names are not easily identifiable from the Electoral Register. One way to overcome this difficulty is to compare those with Asian names which are identifiable from the register with those of non-Asians, and compare the results with the outcome of visible identification at polling booths as voters come out. No doubt there could be a small margin of error in identifying the name and the ethnic group of some persons. A further way of assessing turnout rates is to ask a sample of all electors on the Electoral Register to recall whether they voted at any particular elections and the results can then be compared with the turnout usually recorded by polling clerks. The results of several such exercises, both local and national, are presented below to demonstrate the similarities and differences between the different groups. The detailed results used in this section are presented in chronological order to make it easier for the reader.

A study in 1966 showed very low levels of turnout among Asians in Bradford (Le Lohe 1975). The maximum turnout among Asians in the local elections was 13 per cent in one ward, compared with the highest, 27 per cent, for non-Asians from the wards covered in those surveys.

Another study undertaken in Rochdale in 1968 when the Liberals nominated a Pakistani as their candidate (this election took place soon after Enoch Powell's 'rivers of blood' speech) showed that the turnout among Pakistanis had increased and it appeared that they became both diligent voters and devoted Liberals (Le Lohe and Goldman 1969).

In the 1972 Rochdale parliamentary by-election, it was observed that the Asian turnout was higher compared with previous elections (Anwar 1973). The same pattern was observed in Rochdale in the 1973 local elections when three Pakistanis (two Liberals and one Labour) were contesting in the local council elections (Anwar 1974a). Special efforts were made to mobilize Pakistani voters. One Pakistani was elected for the Liberal party to the council.

In Bradford, in the local elections of 1969, a major attempt was made to mobilize the Asian electorate, partly because an Asian had been nominated as a Liberal candidate. All eight polling stations in Manningham ward were observed and the turnout for Asians was calculated as 53.8 per cent compared with 31.4 per cent for non-Asians. At every subsequent election observed in Bradford, the Asian level of turnout has been consistently higher than that of other people (Le Lohe 1975, 1982). One reason has been the presence of Asian candidates in some elections since 1969, which has taught Asians why, where, and how to vote and made them realize the potential importance of their voting. Asians, for example, stood as Independent candidates in two wards as early as 1963 for local elections. Even then the Asian turnout was 60.9 per cent compared with 43.1 per cent for non-Asians.

In addition to these local studies, three general elections – October 1974, 1979, and 1983 – were monitored to see the turnout patterns for ethnic minorities and particularly for Asians at a national level. The results of these surveys are presented below.

October 1974 general election

Two areas, Bradford and Rochdale, were selected for study to monitor ethnic minority turnout compared with that of whites. Three polling stations in Rochdale were observed and 2,501 people gave their electoral numbers as against 2,543 voters shown in the official returns (under Rule 51 of the Local Election Rules 1973, marked Electoral Registers could be purchased). Thus we had the names of 98.3 per cent of those voting. Inspection of the register showed that 1,576 of the 4,488 electors had Asian names. Since 910 of the voters were Asians, the turnout rate amongst Asians was calculated as 57.7 per cent. Including the 11 Afro-Caribbeans observed to vote with the rest of the electors, the non-Asian turnout level was calculated as 54.6 per cent. But while Asians had a higher turnout rate than other voters from the same area, compared with the previous elections in the same area the Asian turnout was lower. This was due to the intimidation of Asian voters by the National Front who were also contesting that election in the same constituency (Anwar 1975).

Several Asians told the author at the time that they were reluctant to go to the polling stations because of the prospect of being challenged by polling agents for the National Front candidate. These agents were using an almost forgotten provision of the electoral law allowing a candidate to appoint agents who are entitled to sit in the polling station and to ask the presiding officer to put two questions to intending voters designed to establish their identity and confirm that they have not already voted. This had happened at the Rochdale parliamentary by-election in 1972 and the subsequent local and parliamentary elections (Anwar 1973, 1974a, 1975). Although the Returning Officer had arranged for a greater number of polling stations, fear of intimidation certainly reduced the willingness of some Asian voters to go to the polling stations. Those who had language difficulties were particularly reluctant to face these questions. Thus, many Asians were not able to use their civic right to vote.

Table 15 *Asian and non-Asian turnout in the 1970 and 1974 general elections*

| | 1970 | | 1974 | |
| | Asian | Non-Asian | Asian | Non-Asian |
Polling station	%	%	%	%
KB	69.7	55.9	71.1	71.6
KD	71.9	48.0	83.2	61.5
LF	66.8	57.4	76.4	61.7
LG (BH)	67.2	46.3	75.3	53.8
LH (GF)	60.1	46.7	82.1	37.6
LD	—	—	70.5	60.7
KC	—	—	72.9	67.6

Source: Le Lohe 1975.

The Bradford survey also confirmed the high turnout in the general election of 1974. *Table 15* shows the details. It also gives details of the 1970 general election to show the consistently high turnout among Asians.

1979 general election

In the 1979 general election the CRE undertook research to look at turnout rates at certain polling stations in 19 parliamentary constituencies by counting the number of Asian and non-Asian voters who left the polling booths after casting their votes, and comparing the results with the relevant entries in the Electoral Register. The results are presented in *Table 16*.

It is clear from this that the Asian turnout was higher in 18 of the 19 polling districts within constituencies listed compared with that of the non-Asians. Further, in order to see whether this pattern applied to polling stations within constituencies, eight selected polling stations in the three constituencies of Bradford West, Burnley, and Rochdale were covered at the same election. Once again it was confirmed by the findings that the level of turnout among Asians was higher than that of non-Asian voters (73.1 per cent compared with 56.5 per cent), as *Table 17* illustrates.

To look at this tendency for Asians to turn out for elections more than non-Asians, we monitored another type of election, the European Parliament election in June 1979 (Anwar 1980a). It was discovered that the

Table 16 *Turnout in selected constituencies: Asians vs Non-Asians – 1979 general election*

Constituency	Asians			Non-Asians			Totals		
	Electors	Voters	%	Electors	Voters	%	Electors	Voters	%
1. Wandsworth/Battersea	214	147	69	1,316	708	54	1,530	855	56
2. Manchester Ardwick	166	148	89	1,127	673	60	1,293	821	64
3. Wolverhampton South West	223	181	81	939	589	63	1,162	770	67
4. Birmingham Sparkbrook	614	503	82	924	500	55	1,538	1,003	66
5. Bradford West	517	362	70	523	237	46	1,040	599	58
6. City of London and Westminster South	25	19	76	1,256	727	58	1,281	746	59
7. Preston North	459	352	77	1,196	779	66	1,655	1,131	69
8. Nuneaton	247	233	95	933	615	66	1,180	848	72
9. Sheffield Heeley	19	9	48	776	460	60	795	469	59
10. Newcastle North	345	278	81	2,188	1,302	60	2,533	1,580	63
11. Southampton Itchen	590	479	82	2,074	1,201	58	2,664	1,680	63
12. Bristol North East	192	160	84	1,584	1,064	68	1,776	1,224	69
13. Walsall South	458	383	84	517	317	62	975	700	72
14. Brent East	153	145	95	1,671	1,092	66	1,824	1,237	68
15. Leicester South	820	743	91	1,191	718	61	2,011	1,461	73
16. Rochdale	958	693	73	1,570	1,009	65	2,528	1,702	68
17. Glasgow Central	57	43	76	789	410	52	846	453	54
18. Hackney North and Stoke Newington	70	50	72	790	550	70	860	600	70
19. Haringey Hornsey	68	52	77	1,232	854	70	1,300	906	70

Table 17 *Asian and non-Asian turnout in Bradford West, Burnley, and Rochdale – 1979 general election*

Polling station	Asian electors	Non-Asian electors	Asian pro-portion %	Asian voters	Asian turnout %	Non-Asian voters	Non-Asian turnout %
Bradford Drummond	773	398	66.0	531	68.9	206	51.8
Bradford Grange	1,692	1,894	47.2	1,333	78.8	998	52.7
Bradford St Andrews	332	253	56.7	185	55.7	162	64.0
Bradford Southbrook	1,093	2,006	35.3	821	75.1	905	45.1
Bradford (4) Av Totals	3,890	4,551	46.1	2,870	73.8	2,271	49.9
Burnley Stoneyholme	472	1,038	31.2	355	75.2	729	70.2
Rochdale West St	326	285	53.4	199	61.0	187	65.6
Rochdale Silver St	137	1,135	10.8	112	81.8	735	64.8
Rochdale Shepherd	581	477	54.9	415	71.4	308	64.6
Total/Av (8) above	5,406	7,486	42.0	3,951	73.1	4,230	56.5

Asian turnout in Bradford and Burnley (for four polling stations monitored) was higher than non-Asians – 38.5 per cent compared with 21.3 per cent. It is indeed significant that, while the turnout rate among all electors nationally for the European Parliament election was lower than their turnout rate for the general election a month earlier, the turnout rate among Asians was not only higher than that of their non-Asian neighbours who voted at the same polling stations, but also higher than the national turnout rate of 32.1 per cent. Their turnout rate of 38.5 per cent was almost twice that of their non-Asian neighbours and this rate was achieved at an election which the general electorate clearly did not consider to be as important as the general election a month previously.

So far, we have looked at Asian turnout compared with the non-Asians because of the methodological difficulties mentioned above (p. 53). But it is possible to use the *recall* method for other ethnic minority groups by asking whether people voted at a particular election. Using this method, 2,141 male voters in the central constituency of Nottingham were asked if they could recall voting in the general election of 1966; 69 per cent remembered that they *actually* voted which is similar to the actual turnout rate (recorded by polling clerks) of 67.7 per cent. Although few ethnic minorities were included in that survey, nevertheless, 87.9 per cent of Asians, 70.8 per cent of West Indians, and 68.3 per cent of white voters claimed to have voted. Another survey of voters in a Lambeth Central local by-election in March, 1979 showed that West Indian turnout was higher than that of white voters. However, this was a local as distinct from a national election (Anwar 1980a).

Local elections 1980–82

The CRE sponsored further research into the participation of ethnic minorities in the British political process in 1980–81. Some of the findings of this research are used in later parts of the book but here we look at those that relate to turnout only (Le Lohe 1984). Two wards in Ealing, Northcote and Glebe, were looked at in the May 1981 local elections. The returns showed that Asian turnout was almost double that of the non-Asian voters. As *Table 18* shows, the electorate with Asian names was estimated at about 76 per cent but the Asian voters formed 84.9 per cent of the total who cast their votes at this election. Similarly, at Glebe ward the estimated number of Asians on the Electoral Register was about 58 per cent but they formed almost 70 per cent of the voters at this election. This way, the significance of Asians as voters increases when their turnout rate in some areas is consistently almost twice as much as that of the non-Asians.

Table 18 *Turnout rates for Asians and Non-Asians in Ealing – 1981 local elections*

Polling district	Asians			Non-Asians		
	Voters No.	*Electors* No.	%	*Voters* No.	*Electors* No.	%
YA	1,692	2,886	58.6	236	674	35.0
YB	791	1,350	58.6	268	864	31.0
YC	1,167	1,937	60.2	143	437	32.7
Ward total	3,650	6,173	59.1	647	1,975	32.8

Note: The overall turnout in Greater London in this election was 44.4 per cent.

At the same time one ward in Rochdale, Central and Falinge, showed that Asian turnout was 44.2 per cent compared with 28.8 per cent for non-Asians. A similar trend of high turnout rates among Asians was found by looking at the data over three years, 1980, 1981, and 1982, for the University ward of Bradford. Details are given in *Table 19*, which shows a consistent pattern of high level of turnout among Asians.

Table 19 *Turnout rates for Asians and non-Asians – University ward Bradford, May 1980, 1981, and 1982 local elections*

	Asians			Non-Asians		
	Voters	Electors		Voters	Electors	
Year of Election	No.	No.	%	No.	No.	%
1980	3,596	6,879	52.3	1,815	7,539	24.1
1981	3,084	6,621	46.6	1,725	7,209	23.9
1982	3,874	6,635	58.4	1,683	7,293	23.1

Source: Le Lohe 1984.

In this ward, although Asian electors were estimated at less than half the total electorate, they comprised almost two-thirds of those who voted in the elections. This shows that Asians could be more reliable voters and are consequently in a better position to influence the outcome of elections where they vote. *Table 19* shows, at the 1982 local election the Asian turnout rate was two-and-a-half times that of non-Asians.

There were other factors in this election, for example some Asian candidates were standing, which perhaps motivated more Asians to come out to vote. But evidence from different areas shows that, even without Asian candidates in a particular election, the Asian turnout is generally higher than non-Asian.

1981 GLC election

We undertook another exercise to measure turnout for different ethnic groups at the GLC election in May 1981 by using three polling districts in separate constituencies with an ethnic mix (for names see p. 49). The results of our survey confirmed once again that the ethnic minority turnout was higher than the race for white voters. We found that in Paddington the turnout of Afro-Caribbeans was 45 per cent, compared to 40 per cent for whites. In Hounslow the Asian turnout was recorded at 52 per cent compared to 39 per cent for whites. Similarly in Walthamstow the Asian and Afro-Caribbean turnout was higher than whites (40 per cent, 54 per cent, and 37 per cent respectively). It is relevant here to point out that the successful Labour candidate in this constituency, Paul Boateng, was of Afro-Caribbean origin, and this might have created an incentive for ethnic minority voters, particularly the Afro-Caribbeans, to come out and vote in greater numbers.

1983 general election

Twenty constituencies were monitored at the 1983 general election to look at the turnout of different ethnic groups (Anwar 1984a). Some of these constituencies were those that were covered in the 1979 survey referred to above. Interviewers recorded the total number of voters leaving the polling stations, as well as their ethnic group. The relevant electoral registers were checked by an Asian interviewer who estimated the number of Asian and non-Asian names appearing there. A second Asian person checked at random seven constituencies and a very good level of agreement between those two persons was obtained. It is quite possible, however, that the number of Asian names on the Electoral Register was underestimated, because some Asians have anglicized names.

At this election, 81 per cent of Asian voters turned out to vote compared to 60 per cent for non-Asian voters.[4] Almost a quarter of the electors on the register in the areas surveyed were Asian, and the greater likelihood of their turning out to vote suggests that they had a significant impact on the final outcome in each constituency. *Table 20* shows the results of Asian and non-Asian turnout in June 1983. It also shows the results of the 1979 general election survey. In 18 of the 20 constituencies in the table, turnout among Asian voters was higher than among non-Asians. In 1979 the Asian turnout was higher in 18 of the 19 constituencies monitored compared with that of non-Asian voters (see *Table 16*, p. 56).

Although the base numbers are small to draw any firm conclusions, there appears to be no evidence from our results that turnout among Asians was higher in the constituencies where Asians or other ethnic minority candidates stood in the 1983 general election compared with those constituencies where they did not stand.

Table 20 Turnout in selected constituencies: Asian vs non-Asians — 1983 and 1979 General Elections

	Total voters: 1983		Total			Asian				Non-Asian			
	Unweighted* Base	Weighted† Base	electors 1983	1983 %	1979 %	Voters¶ 1983	Electors 1983	1983 %	1979 %	Voters¶ 1983	Electors 1983	1983 %	1979 %
1. Battersea	779	1,097	1,320	60	56	183	225	81	69	914	1,595	57	54
2. Birmingham Ladywood	688	710	1,113	64	—	330	385	86	—	379	728	52	—
3. Birmingham Sparkbrook	446	453	771	59	66	247	355	70	82	206	416	50	55
4. Bradford West	469	553	928	60	58	314	479	66	70	239	449	53	46
5. Brent East	791	1,163	1,809	64	68	106	142	75	95	1,057	1,667	63	66
6. Bristol East	1,891	2,907	4,319	67	69	401	438	92	84	2,506	3,881	65	68
7. Ealing Acton	529	648	925	70	—	52	56	93	—	597	869	69	—
8. Ealing Southall	3,032	2,651	3,613	73	—	2,422	3,026	80	—	229	587	39	—
9. Hertfordshire West	1,621	1,451	2,018	72	—	18	35	51	—	1,433	1,983	73	—
10. Leicester South	1,601	1,561	2,239	78	73	705	872	81	91	856	1,367	63	61
11. Manchester Central	747	948	1,541	62	—	270	335	81	—	678	1,206	56	—
12. Manchester Gorton	759	861	1,442	60	64	152	182	84	89	709	1,260	56	60
13. Newcastle on Tyne Central	1,128	1,128‡	1,914	59	63	174	287	61	81	954	1,627	59	60
14. Newham North West	1,052	1,384	2,198	63	—	599	686	87	—	785	1,512	52	—
15. Norwood	995	1,301	2,121	61	—	35	44	80	—	1,266	2,077	61	—
16. Rochdale	1,162	1,409	2,209	64	68	685	821	83	73	724	1,388	52	65
17. Sheffield Heeley	542	528	901	59	59	9	24	38	48	519	877	59	60
18. Southampton Itchen	1,456	1,774	2,820	63	63	545	580	94	82	1,229	2,240	55	58
19. Walsall South	557	591	842	70	72	242	314	77	84	349	528	66	62
20. Wolverhampton South West	674	789	1,194	66	67	220	268	82	81	569	926	61	63
	20,919	23,907	36,737	65	65	7,709	9,554	81	80	16,198	27,183	60	61

* Turnout recorded by interviewers.   ‡ No official turnout for polling station available.

† Official turnout.   ¶ Grossed up figures.

5 Voting patterns by ethnic groups

The first part of this chapter deals with the voting patterns of different ethnic groups, including whites, in some general elections. The analysis also includes expressed voting intentions for the 1974, 1979, and 1983 general elections and the reasons for voting for a particular party. A comparative analysis in some constituencies will help to record changes at constituency level, as well as to see national trends over a period, based on ethnic groups. The second part covers the voting patterns in a number of local elections over a period of several years. Once again, this analysis will help to look at changes which have taken place over a period in some local areas. We start with the 1972 parliamentary by-election in Rochdale.

Parliamentary elections

The 1972 parliamentary by-election in Rochdale presented an interesting case of ethnic minority participation. The part played by the Pakistanis, it appeared, was a decisive factor in the election result (Anwar 1973). The election and its aftermath brought the social relationships of different ethnic groups into focus in a political context. The role of the candidate of the British Campaign to Stop Immigration (BCSI), Jim Merrick, which led to a social conflict, had been given some attention. This particular conflict united the Pakistanis. The presence of Merrick and the nature of the campaign led ultimately to a realization among Pakistanis that they should act together. Apart from Merrick (BCSI), the other candidates in this by-election were Cyril Smith (Liberal), Lawrence Cunliffe (Labour), and David Trippier (Conservative).

Cyril Smith contested the 1970 general election as a Liberal and came in second to the successful candidate, J. McCann (Labour). After the death of McCann, Smith was the obvious candidate for the by-election.

According to his agent at the time, it was the ethnic minority vote, mainly Pakistanis, that made the difference in the previous general election of 1970. That is why, before Cyril Smith was officially announced as the candidate for the Liberal party, he had held informal meetings with the Pakistani community. Other parties had not chosen their candidates up to that point. Consequently, Lawrence Cunliffe (Labour) conducted a comparatively short campaign and did not have much direct contact with the Pakistani community. David Trippier (Conservative) also did not appear to have much contact with the Pakistanis and, on one occasion, offended them by saying that he was 'amazed to see the socialist and Liberal candidates courting the immigrant vote: it is quite disgusting the way they treat Rochdale immigrants as political illiterates. It is quite like horse trading rather than treating them as individuals. They are taking an amazingly patronising attitude towards them' (*Rochdale Observer*, 25 October 1972). On the other hand, Merrick had the effect of making the Pakistanis, the largest ethnic minority group in the town, take a more active part in the election in order to counter his racialist campaign (Anwar 1979b).

The Labour party workers at this election believed that Pakistanis usually voted for Labour candidates because most of them were workers and they thus identified themselves with Labour. However, in this by-election this view was proved wrong and the tradition of supporting Labour was broken with a shift from Labour to the Liberals. What were the reasons for this shift?

Pakistani votes are usually mobilized and determined by the candidate's personal contacts, his understanding of the community's social and political structure, and his personal links with the *Biraderi* leaders, formal leaders, and associations. Cyril Smith had used all these networks and this is what had contributed to the shift from Labour to the Liberals. The *Guardian* reported that 'Alderman Smith could win on the strength of a switch in support from Labour to Liberal by the Rochdale Asian community numbering about 6000' (*Guardian*, 23 October 1972). This view was also shared by most national and local newspapers. There were other reasons for the Pakistanis' shift to the Liberals: these are mentioned elsewhere (see Anwar 1979b: 140–43).

With the Pakistani support, Smith won the election with a majority of over 5,000 votes over the Labour candidate, Lawrence Cunliffe. Merrick polled 4,074 votes. This was a surprise for the political parties in a town that had prided itself on its good, even exemplary, record of race relations. Jeremy Thorpe, the Liberal party leader at the time, speaking in Nottingham just after the election, alleged 'appalling intimidation of immigrant voters at the polling stations' but conceded that 'there was a need for more campaigning by all three parties on race relations' (*Guardian*, 28 October 1972).

After the election Cyril Smith made a point of thanking the Pakistani community for its support. It was observed that Pakistanis felt very proud of their role in Smith's victory. Moreover, this whole set of events changed the attitude of the Pakistani leadership, which had been divided to a certain extent before the election. As a consequence of this election and the anti-immigrant campaign by the BCSI candidate, they started a 'movement of unity' because they saw that if they were united they would gain more respect.

At the February 1974 general election, both the Labour and Liberal parties worked hard to gain Pakistani support in Rochdale. Meetings were held with them in the community and at work, and campaign literature in Urdu was distributed. However, it appeared that Pakistanis supported in greater numbers the Liberal candidate, Cyril Smith, who won the election with a majority of 8,899. This was confirmed by Lawrence Cunliffe, the Labour candidate, after the results were announced: 'Alderman Smith, in the main, had increased his majority because he got 95 per cent of the immigrant vote' (*Rochdale Observer*, 2 March 1974). Some people believed that Smith's nationwide popularity and his television and radio broadcasts at the time were also an advantage which contributed towards his increased majority at this election. It was observed that Pakistanis felt proud of their support whenever Smith was on the television or in the news. But for his part, Cyril Smith also maintained a close contact with the Pakistanis, listened to their problems sympathetically at special regular surgeries, and attended their functions. Moreover, Pakistanis were appointed as polling agents on behalf of the Liberal party and were sent to attend the Liberal party conference in 1974. This pattern continued later on. Efforts were also made by the Labour and Conservative parties to attract Pakistani support (Anwar 1979b).

The view was expressed in some quarters during the October 1974 general election campaign that the ethnic minority vote as a whole, especially in some 'marginals'[1] such as Bolton West, Gravesend, Preston North, Nelson and Colne, Leicester East, Leicester South, Nottingham East, and Bradford West could be important for the candidates in particular and for the political parties in general. For example, the *Daily Jang*, an Urdu newspaper, reported that the National Front campaign against the Pakistanis in Bolton had disturbed the atmosphere with its demands for the expulsion of all coloured immigrants and that the Pakistani vote could sway the election results (*Daily Jang*, 3 September 1974). Similarly, the *Morning Star* reported that the ethnic minority vote was crucial to defeat the Tories. 'Black and Brown people in Britain will play a decisive part in getting Labour back into power on 4 October' (*Morning Star*, 27 September 1974). For example, there were 16,000 members of ethnic minorities in Leicester South, a constituency of 72,000 voters, and ethnic minority votes, mainly Asian, were very important in changing the February majority of 1,766 for the sitting Conservative MP (*Daily Telegraph*, 2 October 1974). It was reported in the Asian press that the 10 per cent of ethnic minorities living in Gravesend could play a decisive role in the local constituency, one which was regarded as an indication of results in the country as a whole (*Daily Jang*, 4 October 1974). This also applied to other areas where ethnic minority concentrations had maximized their voting importance, particularly in the marginal seats where every vote counted.

It was partly for this reason that the Community Relations Commission (CRC), later replaced by the Commission for Racial Equality (CRE), decided to monitor the participation of the ethnic minorities in the general election of October 1974. This project included a survey of voting intentions and actual voting on the election day. But, before we look at the results concerning voting patterns, it would be useful to look at the data collected between 1970 and 1974 at different intervals in 22 surveys by Harris Polls specifying at least electors' ethnic group and their voting intentions. The question asked in all these surveys was: 'If a general election were held today, how do you think you would vote?'. By dividing the data into three time periods, it was possible to see if there had been changes over time in voting intentions. It must be pointed out that the ethnic minority samples are relatively small but the results help us to look at the trends. Details are presented in *Table 21*.

Over this period as a whole, the figures show that the ethnic minorities had a strong tendency to support Labour compared with white people but with an important minority supporting the Conservative and Liberal parties, particularly between December 1973 and October 1974. This was the period when, as pointed out above, other parties had realized the importance of the ethnic minority vote and had started making efforts to get this vote for their particular parties. The sharp rise in Liberal support, both among whites and ethnic minorities, between December 1973 and October 1974 (shown in *Table 21*) is a reflection of the Liberal party revival at that time.

Table 21 *Voting intentions between June 1970 and October 1974*

Period of surveys	Ethnic group	Number interviewed	Lab. %	Con. %	Lib. %	Others %
June–December 1970	Whites	8,000	48	44	7	1
	Ethnic minorities	115	69	25	5	1
February–July 1971	Whites	10,311	51	41	7	1
	Ethnic minorities	166	80	17	2	1
December 1973– October 1974	Whites	13,835	40	37	20	2
	Ethnic minorities	285	63	23	13	1

Source: Adapted from Anwar and Kohler 1975.

In the CRC survey of the 1974 October general election, this trend of strong support among ethnic minorities for the Labour party was confirmed. But it also showed that the ethnic minorities' support could be attracted by other parties, as in the case of Rochdale. *Table 22* gives details of voting patterns of white and ethnic minority voters by using mock ballots in six constituencies.

Table 22 *Voting patterns by ethnic group – October 1974 general election*

Constituency	Ethnic group	Number interviewed (=100%)	Con. %	Lab. %	Lib. %	Others %
Birmingham Sparkbrook	Whites	41	29	68	3	—
	Ethnic minorities	110	3	90	7	—
Bradford West	Whites	39	15	82	3	—
	Ethnic minorities	25	20	72	8	—
Brent East	Whites	31	26	64	10	—
	Ethnic minorities	53	15	72	13	—
Croydon North-East	Whites	37	30	40	30	—
	Ethnic minorities	28	11	64	25	—
Lambeth Norwood	Whites	40	25	52	23	—
	Ethnic minorities	21	5	81	9	5
Leicester South	Whites	40	52	30	10	8
	Ethnic minorities	76	16	83	1	—

Source: Anwar and Kohler 1975.

It must be pointed out that the majority of these constituencies were Labour-held at the time of our survey. In two special surveys conducted in Rochdale and Bradford West by Dr Le Lohe, the following voting patterns emerged among Asian voters (see *Table 23*).

Table 23 *Voting patterns among Asians – February and October 1974 general elections*

		Lib. %	Lab. %	Con. %	Others %
Rochdale	February 1974	55	40	5	—
	October 1974	50	46	4	—
Bradford West	February 1974	3	61	34	2
	October 1974	1	80	19	—

Source: Anwar and Kohler 1975.

Further information about the swing towards Labour came from the CRC survey in the seven constituencies before the October election. Respondents were asked who they voted for in the February 1974 election and who they intended to support in the October 1974 election. Both were based on respondents' stated actions and so are reasonably comparable.

It is clear from *Table 24* that slightly more people expressed a party preference in October than recalled their vote in February, but the answers show a swing (3 per cent) to Labour amongst white voters in line with the national trend. However, the swing to Labour amongst Afro-Caribbean and Asian voters (7.5 per cent) was more pronounced.

This evidence clearly demonstrates the swing towards Labour among the minorities between the two elections, but more important, it also demonstrates that other parties can attract support from minorities if they try. In particular, the Liberals' share of the vote, both among whites and ethnic minorities, increased following the trend in British politics during that period. Rochdale is a good example for demonstrating the increase in their support.

The October 1974 results should be seen in the context of the views of both ethnic minorities and whites towards the government, which was Labour. They were therefore asked about their satisfaction with the government in running the country and then about their party preference for voting in the February and October 1974 general elections. Well over half (57 per cent) of the ethnic minority sample felt satisfied with the way

Table 24 *Party supported in February and October 1974 general elections*

A. *Which party did you vote for in February?*

	Whites (353) %	Ethnic minorities (335) %	Afro-Caribbean (116) %	Asian (219) %
Labour	41	47	45	49
Conservative	23	9	4	11
Liberal	13	7	2	1

B. *Which party are you most inclined to support now? (October)*

	Whites %	Ethnic minorities %	Afro-Caribbean %	Asian %
Labour	45	63	66	61
Conservative	25	10	6	12
Liberal	14	9	3	11

Source: Anwar and Kohler 1975.

the Labour government had been running the country, while 19 per cent felt that they had been doing 'a bad job'. Although the sample of ethnic minorities was small, it gave some indications in this respect. In contrast to the views of the ethnic minorities, more white respondents felt that the government had been doing 'a bad job' (42 per cent) compared with those saying it had been doing 'a good job' (39 per cent). See *Table 25* for details.

Table 25 *Attitudes towards government*

	Total (4,343) %	Whites (4,257) %	Ethnic minorities (86) %
Good job	39	39	57
Bad job	42	42	19
Don't know	19	19	24

Source: Anwar and Kohler 1975.

Table 26 *Party preferences – 1974 survey*

	Total (4,343) %	Whites (4,257) %	Ethnic minorities (86) %
Conservative better	30	30	13
Conservative worse	41	41	45
Don't know	29	29	42

Source: Anwar and Kohler 1975.

Only 13 per cent of the ethnic minorities thought the Conservatives would do a better job. Forty-five per cent thought they would do a worse job. However, 42 per cent had no opinion about the matter or thought they would be no better or no worse. Whites also felt (*Table 26*) that the Conservatives would do a worse job, but the feeling was less marked than it was among the ethnic minorities (41 per cent Conservative worse and 30 per cent Conservative better). A fairly high proportion of the ethnic minorities (42 per cent) were unable to say anything one way or the other, or thought that the Conservatives would be no better or no worse.

One should not forget that some of the constituencies included in the survey were Labour strongholds. Labour support in large numbers among the ethnic minorities was also confirmed by the voting pattern in the February 1974 general election, as shown in *Table 27*.

Table 27 *Voting patterns – general election, February 1974*

		Total (4,343) %	Whites (4,257) %	Ethnic minorities (86) %
No – did not vote		11	11	11
Yes – voted:	Labour	36	36	52
	Conservative	30	31	11
	Liberal	13	13	8
	Nationalist	2	2	—
	Other party	*	*	—
	Refused	4	4	8
	Can't remember	4	3	10

Source: Anwar and Kohler 1975.

Two constituencies which showed varying support for the Labour Party were Rochdale and Bradford West. In both constituencies, suggestions were made that the Labour party had supported Bangladesh in the conflict with West Pakistan in 1971, and the Pakistanis tended not to support Labour as a consequence. There were other factors as well, as mentioned above, in relation to the Pakistanis' support for the Liberals in Rochdale. In Bradford West the real contest was between the Conservative candidate, the sitting MP John Wilkinson, and the Labour candidate, Edward Lyons. Both of them had shown considerable interest in ethnic minority affairs to win ethnic minority (mainly Asian) support, as the electoral calculations in the constituency showed that the Asian vote was crucial.

In appealing for Asian support, John Wilkinson had an important advantage, for the largest section of the Asian electorate was from what was then called West Pakistan. Wilkinson was able to associate himself with West Pakistan during the 1971 India–Pakistan war. He justified the action of the army in East Pakistan and compared it to the position of the British army in Northern Ireland (*Telegraph and Argus*, 17 September 1971). Various prominent members of the Pakistani community had previously announced that they were switching their support to the Conservatives because some Labour MPs were making distorted statements about events in what was then East Pakistan (*Telegraph and Argus*, 8 May 1971).

It appears that one political decision that affected Wilkinson's support among Pakistanis was the withdrawal of Pakistan from the Commonwealth, as a consequence of which Pakistanis had to register under the Pakistan Act of 1973 in order to continue as electors. There was a lot of confusion about this and many Pakistanis failed to register, as was clear from the Electoral Register which came into force on 15 February 1974 which showed a reduction in the number of Asian names from 10,991 to 6,976. There was a significant reduction in the potential Pakistani vote and therefore in Wilkinson's support. This was confirmed by Wilkinson after his defeat. He said that without the Pakistan Act and the Liberal intervention he would have won with a substantial majority (*Telegraph and Argus*, 1 March 1974). Many observers believed that this was true. Several Pakistanis from Bradford and elsewhere told the author at the time that they were 'really sorry' about John Wilkinson's defeat as he was a very strong supporter of Pakistan and Pakistanis in this country.

In the October 1974 general election Labour's local efforts to recapture the Pakistani vote in Bradford and Rochdale appeared to be greatly helped by the actions of the new Labour government. There was positive evidence that the new government was more sympathetic to the ethnic minorities and this seemed to make Labour candidates acceptable, where previously they had felt unwelcome. Edward Lyons was now the sitting MP for Bradford West and was therefore in a position to help his ethnic minority constituents and forge relationships which brought support for him in the next election. This trend was confirmed by a survey in the constituency of the voting behaviour of Asians. It showed that on the basis of recalled behaviour in Bradford West, there was an estimated swing of 12 per cent among Asian voters from the Conservative to the Labour candidate. Similarly a small swing of 6 per cent took place in Rochdale from the Liberal candidate to Labour, but the Liberal party still held on to the majority of the Pakistani vote. The reasons for this are mentioned in some detail elsewhere (Anwar 1979b).

The next opportunity to look at voting patterns at a general election came in May 1979. This time the local elections and the general election were held on the same day. There were some pre-election surveys which showed voting intentions. The CRE survey included 1,138 respondents who were asked about their voting intentions at the general election. The majority of the respondents (52 per cent) intended to vote for the Labour party, 23 per cent for the Conservatives, while only 6 per cent expressed an intention to vote for the Liberal party (see *Table 28*).

Further analysis of the expressed intentions of voters showed that it was primarily those aged 55 and over among all ethnic groups who expressed an intention to vote for the Conservative party.

Having established party loyalties, we went on to look at respondents' reasons for supporting a particular party. Let us look first at their reasons for supporting Labour. Given that just over one in two respondents intended to vote for the Labour party, it was important to establish the reasons why they held this preference.

Table 28 *Voting intentions by race – 1979 general election*

	Total (1,138) %	White (582) %	Afro-Caribbean (144) %	Asian (397) %
Labour	52	39	66	65
Conservative	23	37	6	9
Liberal	6	8	8	3

The main reasons were as follows:

1 'They are for the working class' (28 per cent).
2 'Generally like them/think they are better (16 per cent).
3 'Always voted Labour' (13 per cent).
4 'Labour has achieved a lot/should let them continue' (13 per cent).
5 'They are sympathetic towards immigrants/will solve problems of immigration' (9 per cent).
6 'They are helpful/good for ethnic minorities' (5 per cent).

Other reasons were mentioned by fewer than 5 per cent of respondents.

There were few differences between various groups in their responses with the notable exception of those referring to the Labour party's 'sympathy' for problems associated with immigrants. Here, 12 per cent of Afro-Caribbean voters and 15 per cent of Asian voters expressed this view while no white voter did so.

A similar analysis of the 23 per cent of all respondents who intended to vote for the Conservative party produced the following main reasons:

1 'Generally like/think the Conservatives are better' (26 per cent).
2 'Labour has been in power too long/long enough' (12 per cent).
3 'Conservatives want a cut in taxes' (8 per cent).
4 'Comments pro Mrs Thatcher' (7 per cent).

However, an expressed intention to vote for a particular party is only a very general indication of the orientation of voters. How likely is it that such expressed intentions will be translated into action? In order to explore this, we asked our respondents to indicate the likelihood of their actually voting for the candidates put up by the party of their choice in the general election. Eighty-two per cent of those who had expressed an intention to vote for the Labour party thought it 'extremely' or 'very' likely that they would actually vote Labour on the day. And among these, white voters and those who were older than 35 years of age (holding ethnic group constant) were 'extremely' or 'very' likely actually to vote for their Labour candidate. There were too few Conservative party supporters (in terms of expressed intentions) to enable a similar analysis to be undertaken. Two-thirds of ethnic minority respondents who did not actually intend to turn out to vote for their Labour candidates expressed no reasons for not doing so, while white voters not intending to do the same thing expressed various reasons for their views (such as the Labour party's poor record with the trades unions, 22 per cent; their past record generally, 20 per cent; and their apparently too left-wing attitude, 10 per cent).

Table 29 *Party voted for in October 1974 general election analysed by voting intentions in 1979*

Base: All those claimed voting in October 1974 Voted for in 1974 election	Intended to vote for Labour 1979			Intended to vote for Conservative 1979		
	White (175) %	Afro-Car. (40) %	Asian (158) %	White (165) %	Afro-Car. (7) %	Asian (22) %
Labour	92	98	96	23	43	59
Conservative	4	3	2	72	57	36
Liberal	2	—	1	2	—	5
Other party	2	—	1	3	—	—
Refused	1	—	—	1	—	—

A further dimension of voting intentions can be gleaned from a comparison of the political parties for which respondents voted in 1974 and their voting intentions in the 1979 general election. This comparison is presented in *Table 29*.

The voting intentions which were expressed by respondents in 1979 were likely to result in voting behaviour in line with those intentions. Although the numbers of Afro-Caribbeans and Asians who intended to vote for the Conservative party are small, these give some indications of their preferences. Twenty three per cent of white people who intended to vote Conservative in 1979 claimed to have voted Labour in October 1974. On the other hand, 43 per cent of Afro-Caribbeans and 59 per cent of Asians intending to vote for the Conservative party in 1979 claimed to have voted Labour in October 1974. Data from the 1979 Gallup pre-election surveys also help to assess voting by ethnic groups and, within these, the social class. The sample for ethnic minorities is small, as shown in *Table 30*, but it is useful to look at the trends.

Although the support for the Labour party among ethnic minorities is high, it is not as strong as the CRE survey shows it to be. One reason for this is that the CRE surveys were mainly undertaken in inner-city areas where support for the Labour party is usually greater and the Gallup surveys were more widespread. But it must be pointed out that we are still discussing voting intentions, not actual voting.

In the 1979 survey we asked the respondents whether they knew the names of the candidates who were standing in their constituencies for

Table 30 *Voting by social class within ethnic groups – 1979*

Party voted for	Ethnic group								
	Whites social class			Afro-Caribbeans social class			Asians social class		
	A, B, CI (3,588) %	C2 (3,290) %	D, E (3,146) %	A, B, CI (29) %	C2 (37) %	D, E (40) %	A, B, CI (36) %	C2 (32) %	D, E (40) %
Conservative	57	40	32	17	11	15	25	28	25
Labour	20	35	38	41	49	48	42	50	50
Liberal	9	5	5	5	8	3	6	3	0
Non-voter	15	20	25	35	32	35	28	19	25

Source: 1979 Gallup pre-election surveys used by Studlar and Layton-Henry, 1984.

various parties. We discovered that one in two respondents was unaware of the names of any of the candidates in their constituency. Of those who could identify at least one candidate, 46 per cent were white, 35 per cent were Afro-Caribbeans, and 31 per cent were Asians. Generally, Labour candidates were more likely to be correctly identified than candidates of other parties. Among the white respondents, 61 per cent correctly identified their Labour candidate both by name and by party. Among Afro-Caribbeans and Asians this figure was even higher (70 per cent and 64 per cent respectively).

Correct identification of Conservative candidates was much lower; only 24 per cent of both the Asian and white respondents respectively identified their Conservative candidate, whilst this figure was even lower among Afro-Caribbeans (10 per cent). Identification of candidates of other parties was also low. Only 16 per cent of white people and 4 per cent of Asians correctly identified a Liberal candidate, although in Rochdale the Liberal candidate was identified by an overwhelming majority of both white and Asian respondents. It is an important aspect of voting behaviour that electors are aware of the names of candidates and are able to identify their parties in order to make decisions about voting in relation to party policies. It is also important to be aware of the names because they liked a particular candidate, irrespective of his/her party policies. It appears that familiarity with candidates is another important aspect of the voting behaviour of Asians.

Let us look at actual voting patterns. As part of the CRE's 1979 general election survey a sample of voters from 24 constituencies was asked to record (on duplicate 'ballot' papers) the way they voted in the polling stations. The 'ballot' papers were similar to those used in the real election, except that they were marked by the interviewers to record the voter's ethnic group. The 'ballot' papers were placed in a box by the voters as they left the polling booth. Out of a total sample of 3,225 voters involved in this exercise, 1,205 were from ethnic minority groups. The results show that the majority of ethnic minority voters actually voted for the Labour party as against other parties. While 50 per cent of whites voted Labour, 90 per cent of Afro-Caribbeans and 86 per cent of Asians in the sample voted Labour. *Table 31* presents the details.

Among whites in the sample, Labour had an 11 per cent lead over the Conservatives compared with a 78 per cent lead among Asians and 85 per cent among Afro-Caribbeans. This trend of support for the Labour party was similar to that found in 1974. In this regard, while support among whites had decreased marginally from 56 per cent in 1974 to 50 per cent in 1979, it increased by a similar amount among Asians (from 78 per cent in 1974 to 86 per cent in 1979). Support for Labour among Afro-Caribbeans remained roughly the same (89 per cent in 1974 and 90 per cent in 1979). As a group, 86 per cent of ethnic minorities voted Labour, 8 per cent voted Conservative and 5 per cent voted Liberal.

When we compare the 1979 survey results with the 1974 survey referred to above, we find that in the wards in seven constituencies where comparisons of voting were possible, it appeared that the Conservative vote among ethnic minorities, particularly Asians, had increased in 1979 when compared with 1974. It was found that ethnic minority 'swings' to the Conservative party were largely accounted for by the voting pattern of Asian voters as against Afro-Caribbean voters. Whereas Afro-Caribbean

Table 31 *Voting patterns by ethnic group – 1979 general election*

	Total (3,225)		White (2,020)		Asian (871)		Afro-Car. (285)		Other (49)	
	No.	%	No.	%	No.	%	No.	%	No.	%
Voting										
Conservative	883	27	793	39	66	8	14	5	10	20
Labour	2,048	64	1,008	50	750	86	255	90	35	71
Liberal	219	7	161	9	46	5	9	3	3	6
Other parties	75	2	58	2	9	1	7	2	1	2
Labour lead over Conservative	37%		11%		78%		85%		51%	

voters solidly backed the Labour party, Asian voters spread their votes between the Labour and Conservative parties in such a way that higher proportions voted for the Conservative party in some constituencies than in others. In seven constituencies out of the 24 we surveyed, over 15 per cent of Asian voters cast their votes for the Conservative party, as *Table 32* shows.[2]

One of the local election surveys between the two elections, and before Mrs Thatcher's 'swamping' remarks, showed increasing support among Asians for the Conservative party. Some of this was clearly achieved by the individual candidates taking more interest in race relations and ethnic minorities in general, and some by the efforts of the Conservative Central Office and the Anglo-Asian and Anglo-West Indian Conservative societies. The Conservative party put forward two Asian candidates for parliament for the first time (see p. 102), and several Asian candidates to contest local elections. The question that arises, therefore, is how did ethnic minority groups influence the 1979 general election results?

After examining support for the Labour party among ethnic minority voters, it is reasonable to conclude that with an even distribution of the 'ethnic vote' between the two parties, the Conservatives would have won that general election with an even greater majority than they did. On the other hand, ethnic minority voters clearly helped some Labour candidates, such as those who stood in Leicester South and Bradford West, to increase the Labour majority in those constituencies, compared to the October 1974 general election results. There were 87 constituencies in which ethnic minority residents constituted more than 5 per cent of the population. In 41 of these, the total number of ethnic minority residents exceeded the size of the majority of the successful candidate in each of the three general elections (February and October 1974, and May 1979).

Table 32 *Support among Asians for Conservative and Labour candidates in wards in selected constituencies – 1979 general election*

Constituency	% vote for Conservative	% vote for Labour
Lambeth Norwood	40	60
Hornsey Haringey	33	67
Glasgow Central	31	69
Croydon North East	30	60
Ealing Acton	19	81
Newcastle North	18	77
Brent East	16	79

Among these, the Labour party held 24 in the May 1979 general election. It is worth stressing again that it is not only the actual number of ethnic minority voters in some constituencies which makes them 'important', but also their relative concentration, which places them in a position to influence the outcome of elections.

In some constituencies, there were roughly as many ethnic minority voters on the Electoral Register as there were New Commonwealth and Pakistan-born citizens recorded in the 1971 census, as mentioned in Chapter 2. Therefore, the proportion of the total electorate who are ethnic minorities in individual constituencies makes them 'important' and 'influential'.

The importance of the ethnic minority vote was reported widely in the press just before the 1983 general election. For example, *The Times* reported, 'Parties seek ethnic vote but fail to offer minorities safe seats'. It added, 'the ethnic minorities go into the June election with more (ethnic minority candidates standing for the three main parties than in all post-war general elections put together, and with the parties hunting the ethnic minority vote as never before' (*The Times*, 4 June 1983). The main political parties publicized their messages for the ethnic minorities in leaflets translated into various Asian languages, on special posters aimed at them, and through the ethnic minority press.

The Conservative party issued an advertisement headed, 'Labour Says He's Black. Tories Say He's British'. It starts: 'With the Conservatives there are no "blacks", no "whites", just people. Conservatives believe that treating minorities as equals encourages the majority to treat them as equals' (Conservative party, May 1983). This advertisement was attacked by, among others, the Labour leader, Michael Foot.

The surveys about voting intentions confirmed the previous findings of the 1979 general election that an overwhelming majority of ethnic minority voters intended to vote for the Labour party. A poll conducted for London Weekend Television by the Harris Research Centre showed that 65 per cent of Asians and 67 per cent of Afro-Caribbeans intended to vote for the Labour party; 7 per cent of Asians and 5 per cent of Afro-Caribbeans supported the Conservatives; and 7 per cent of Asians and 4 per cent of Afro-Caribbeans hoped to vote for the Alliance (*The Times*, 7 June 1983). Figures for whites were not collected as they were not included in the survey. Another survey, conducted by the Centre for Contemporary Studies among undefined 'black Londoners' for the *Voice* newspaper, showed that 71 per cent of those questioned before the election said they intended to support the Labour party, 8 per cent the

Alliance, and 3 per cent the Conservative party (*The Daily Telegraph,*
7 June 1983). The difficulty with both these surveys was that no white
electors were interviewed for comparative purposes. One important
finding of the Harris survey referred to above was that almost 10 per cent
of Asians between 18 and 24 years of age were intending to vote Conservative, compared with only 3 per cent of the Asians who were over 45
years of age. The Gallup Polls at the 1983 general election showed 21 per
cent of ethnic minorities supporting the Conservative party compared
with 64 per cent and 15 per cent supporting Labour and the Alliance
respectively. Gallup also showed that of all those who supported Labour
at the 1979 general election 31 per cent had changed allegiance in 1983
compared with 21 per cent of ethnic minority Labour supporters. As is
shown below (p. 79) this changed allegiance was reflected in their actual
voting on the election day, as found by the Harris Research Centre's
national exit poll for ITN.

The CRE's survey of the 1983 general election on election day showed
that the support for the Labour party was especially strong among ethnic
minority voters (Anwar 1984a). For example, 81 per cent claimed to have
voted for the Labour party compared with 43 per cent of white voters.
Afro-Caribbeans in particular were more likely to vote Labour (86 per
cent) compared with Asians (80 per cent) and other ethnic minorities (60
per cent) as shown in *Table 33*. The table shows the results obtained from
the exit poll based on 4,240 voters, of whom 52 per cent were white, 14
per cent Afro-Caribbean, 32 per cent Asian, and 2 per cent other ethnic
minorities. Over and above this 16 per cent of all ballot papers collected

Table 33 *Voting patterns by ethnic group: 1983 general election*

	Ethnic group					
	Total (4,240) %	White (2,190) %	All ethnic minority (2,050) %	Afro-Car. (603) %	Asian (1,375) %	Other E.M. (72) %
Labour	48	35	70	72	71	49
Conservative	20	29	6	6	5	22
Alliance	14	17	9	4	11	9
Others	1	1	1	1	1	*
Refused	16	18	13	17	12	19

were refusals, with the oldest age range (55+ years) being those most likely to refuse, a common finding in survey research. Young voters (under 35 years) and Asians were the least likely to refuse.

Excluding those who refused to participate, *Table 34* below shows that 57 per cent of voters in these constituencies voted for the Labour candidates, 24 per cent for the Conservatives, 17 per cent for the Alliance, and 2 per cent for other parties. As a group, 81 per cent of ethnic minority voters supported Labour. This represented a lead of 62 per cent over other parties, compared to a lead of 14 per cent for all voters in these constituencies. It must be pointed out that most of the 25 constituencies covered in this survey were Labour-held at the time of the 1983 general election and this had some bearing on these results. Let us look at the national exit poll which was conducted by the Harris Research Centre for ITN. It too showed that the majority of ethnic minorities had voted Labour (57 per cent) but 24 per cent and 16 per cent of them had voted Conservative and Alliance respectively. It appears that, although the trend was the same nationally (as shown by the ITN–Harris poll), the inner-city areas covered in our survey show more support for Labour among ethnic minorities. This could be explained by the type of constituencies covered in our survey. They are mainly inner-city areas, with higher proportions of working class electors. Fourteen of those constituencies were won by Labour, nine by Conservatives, and one by the Alliance.

In the Harris Research Centre survey those respondents who always or usually voted Labour were asked, 'Why do you normally vote Labour?' Of 258 Afro-Caribbeans and 354 Asians, 76 per cent of Afro-Caribbeans and 64 per cent of Asians respectively said because Labour 'supports the working class'. On the other hand only 7 per cent of Afro-Caribbeans and 31 per cent of Asians said they vote Labour because it 'supports blacks and Asians' (Harris Research Centre 1983). These results show how the Labour party is perceived by ethnic minorities and what relationship this has with their voting patterns.

Two post-election analyses found that the movement away from Labour in areas with ethnic minority concentration was less than in other areas (*Sunday Times*, 12 June 1983). But the comparison of the two CRE surveys showed that the ethnic minority support for Labour had decreased in 1983. See *Table 34* for details.

It is clear from *Table 34* that the Labour lead over other parties had decreased considerably, in the constituencies surveyed, among all ethnic groups and among white voters in particular. Another survey showed that

Table 34 Comparison of voting patterns in 1979 and 1983 general elections

	Total		White		All ethnic minorities		Afro-Caribbean		Asian		Other	
	1983 (3,608) %	1979 (3,225) %	1983 (1,808) %	1979 (2,020) %	1983 (1,800) %	1979 (1,205) %	1983 (513) %	1979 (285) %	1983 (1,229) %	1979 (871) %	1983 (58) %	1979 (49) %
Labour	57	64	43	50	81	86	86	90	80	86	60	71
Conservative	24	27	35	39	7	8	8	5	6	8	27	20
Liberal/Alliance	17	7	21	9	11	5	5	3	12	5	11	6
Other	2	2	2	2	1	1	2	2	1	1	*	2
Labour lead over other parties	+14	+28	−15	0	+62	+72	+71	+80	+61	+72	+22	+43

21 per cent of ethnic minority voters who had voted for the Labour party in 1979 switched from Labour to other parties at the 1983 election (*Guardian*, 13 June 1983). But, in comparison, the Labour vote had remained strongest among Afro-Caribbeans. Only the Liberal/SDP Alliance had substantially increased its share of the vote in these constituencies among both white and ethnic minority voters.[3] The highest recorded ethnic minority vote for the Labour party was in Bristol East (93 per cent), for the Conservatives in Croydon North-East (27 per cent), and for the Alliance in Rochdale (54 per cent). This pattern was consistent with the CRE survey of the 1979 general election referred to above. Monitoring of these three constituencies has shown that the personal popularity of the respective candidates for these parties was one of the key factors in attracting the ethnic minority vote.

Local elections

The most comprehensive work on ethnic minority participation in local elections has been undertaken by Mich Le Lohe in Bradford. His monitoring of the Asian participation in elections goes back to the early 1960s (Le Lohe 1975: 84–122). He has demonstrated over the years that Asian turnout is higher than that of the non-Asians, as referred to in the previous chapter. It has also been shown that Asians have voted for the Labour, Conservative, Liberal, and more recently the SDP candidates. Although the general trend has been that the majority of Asians voted Labour, local events and the ethnic origin of the candidates has played an important role in determining support from the local Asians in Bradford. For example, in the District Council elections in May 1982, in the University ward where a Labour Pakistani councillor who had joined the SDP was defending his seat, 37.3 per cent of Asians voted for him whilst 58.9 per cent of those interviewed voted for the Labour candidate (Le Lohe 1982).[4] The SDP candidate won the election. However, it must be pointed out that this was a study of a local area and of a ward with a lot of Asians as electors (see *Table 4*, p. 22), who had history of involvement in this ward's politics. Therefore, based on this evidence, generalizations for the country as a whole or even for Bradford's other wards would be misleading.

The same applies to another area which was studied in the early 1970s, Rochdale, where both the Labour and Liberal parties were active in attracting the Asian vote in local elections. Their efforts included putting forward Asian candidates. In the 1973 Metropolitan District Council elections, two Pakistanis were nominated by the Liberal party from the wards with the highest residential concentrations of Pakistanis, the Central and Falinge ward and the Wardleworth and Newbold ward. This indicated that Pakistanis were seen not only as voters and vote-gatherers but also as capable of being candidates. It was also a recognition of the Pakistani support for the Liberals at the 1972 parliamentary by-election (Anwar 1974a). Once the two Pakistanis were nominated as Liberal candidates, action was taken by the community leadership to mobilize support for them and for the Liberal party. The Liberal candidates were S. H. Syed, a medical doctor, and Karim Dad, the president of the local Pakistan welfare association. The Labour party nominated the sitting Pakistani councillor, A. H. Chowdry, from another ward in Rochdale, Spotland, where there were not many Asian voters.

It was interesting to note that in these three wards only one, Spotland, was contested by one Conservative party candidate (with a three-member ward, there could have been three) and for the other two wards Conservatives had no candidate at all. One could give the simple explanation that these were predominantly the working-class wards and the Conservatives did not have much hope of getting enough support to win these seats. This meant that there was a straight contest between Labour and the Liberals. As a result of the Liberal party support and the Pakistani community campaign and unity, S. H. Syed was elected for the Central and Falinge ward along with two other Liberals, Cyril Smith, MP, and R. H. Stott. As a result, strong candidates like Mrs M. E. Randle, chair of the Rochdale Education Committee, were defeated in this ward. In the other ward, Karim Dad, the Pakistani Liberal candidate for Wardleworth and Newbold ward, was not elected, but he came within approximately 100 votes of the last Labour candidate to be elected, and topped the list of the other Liberal candidates from the same ward. There was no doubt that an overwhelming majority of Pakistanis in this election voted for the Liberal party. In Spotland ward, on the other hand, the Pakistani Labour candidate, A. H. Chowdry, received only 558 votes out of an electorate of 5,675. In this ward, all three Liberals were elected and no Labour or Conservative candidate got more than 500 to 700 votes. The majority of the Asians in this ward had voted for the Liberal party candidates, although a significant minority had voted Labour. This pattern of voting among Asians in Rochdale has continued since 1973; checks made at some local elections in the late 1970s and early 1980s have confirmed this.

On the whole, the number of votes received by the three Pakistani candidates in 1973, both from Asians and non-Asians, showed that they were being accepted as party candidates, as were the ethnic minority candidates in other areas.[5] This is confirmed by the election of several ethnic minority councillors for the main political parties throughout the country, particularly in London. The discussion about the ethnic minority candidates generally, and their performance at some general and local elections in particular, is dealt with in the next chapter.

In summary, the voting patterns in local elections depend on local conditions. However, regular contacts between political parties and ethnic minorities, the mobilization and organization of ethnic minorities at elections, the candidates' personal familiarity with the ethnic minority electors, their party policies generally, and the presence of ethnic minority candidates are important factors in attracting ethnic minority votes.

6 The political parties' response

It is clear from research evidence so far that the policies of political parties that affect ethnic minorities, in particular immigration and race relations issues, are directly related to their voting patterns. The policies and initiatives taken by the political parties to encourage ethnic minority participation in the mainstream political process are crucial. The survey material from the last two general elections concerning the question of ethnic minority participation in British politics is presented in this chapter.

One way to examine the response of the political parties to the question of ethnic minority participation is to look at the number of candidates adopted by the main political parties in national and local elections in the past ten years. What sort of constituencies had they contested? What support did these candidates receive from the party machinery? What success rate did the ethnic minority candidates achieve? Why did a lot of 'independent' and 'fringe' party ethnic minority candidates stand at elections? Do they succeed and how does their success rate compare with that of ethnic minority candidates who stand for the main political parties?

In addition to the 1971 census data, which revealed the concentrations of ethnic minorities in various parts of Britain, it was the report by the Community Relations Commission (CRC) published in 1975, about the participation of ethnic minorities in the general election of October 1974, which drew the attention of the political parties to the importance of ethnic minorities in the political process (Anwar and Kohler 1975). The CRC had continually encouraged members of ethnic minority communities to exercise their right to vote so that their needs would be made known to the political parties and so that the resources required to meet their needs could more readily be made available. This report reviewed the participation of the ethnic minorities in that election, the role of race relations matters in the election, and the activities of overtly anti-immigrant candidates. The study showed (based on the 1971 census figures) that there were 76 constituencies in the February 1974 general election and 85 in the October 1974 general election in which ethnic minorities could make a significant impact on the outcome of results in these elections. The report concluded that the ethnic minorities played a significant part in determining the outcome of the October 1974 general election; they swung more to Labour than the electorate as a whole, at least partly in response to the Labour government's actions to benefit the ethnic minorities. Although most ethnic minority voters conformed with their socio-economic group in voting Labour, other parties were able to attract support among the ethnic minorities where they made the effort; whereas anti-immigrant candidates made little or no progress at the election.

This report attracted a great deal of publicity and made a significant impact in drawing the attention of political parties to the importance of the ethnic minority vote. The ethnic minority leadership and race relations workers used the report to create more awareness among both the political parties and the ethnic minorities themselves. The period between October 1975, when the report was published, and the next general election in 1979 saw several developments in this context. The Nuffield Election Studies had also pointed out the growing electoral importance of the ethnic minority electorate (Butler and Kavanagh 1974, 1975). After the publication of the CRC study, special efforts were made by the three main political parties to recruit ethnic minority members and to encourage them to register. They were also organized and mobilized at election times through their community leaders. Election literature, manifestos, and election addresses were translated into various Asian languages and bilingual party workers were used during election campaigns.

The Conservative party took certain initiatives to encourage the ethnic minorities to join the party after the publication of the above-mentioned studies. In 1976 it set up an ethnic minorities unit in the Conservative Central Office's Department of Community Affairs, headed by Andrew Rowe (now MP). The unit was the responsibility of Mervyn Kohler. Its objective was to make party members aware of the growing electoral importance of Asian and Afro-Caribbean electors and to influence party policy to improve the image of the party among ethnic minorities. One of the first initiatives of the unit was to help form an Anglo-Asian Conservative Society through which to recruit Asians directly into the party. This was followed by the formation of an Anglo-West Indian Conservative Society with the same objective. These societies still exist and have representations on the area and national committees of the National Union of Conservative and Unionist Associations. The Anglo-Asian Conservative Society had 27 local branches throughout the country by the end of 1984.

It appears from the evidence available that the Conservative Central Office gave a high priority to the Anglo-Asian Conservative Society. Mrs Thatcher became its honorary President and William Whitelaw (now Viscount Whitelaw) became one of its 14 honorary vice-presidents. Others included Lord Carrington and Michael Heseltine. Its first chair was councillor Narindar Saroop who contested Greenwich for the Conservative party at the 1979 general election, and who was instrumental in the formation of the society. The society has held meetings and receptions at the party conferences which are attended by a large number of both ministers and MPs.[1] It also holds an annual reception at the House of Commons to introduce its members to MPs and others. This reception was attended by the Prime Minister, Margaret Thatcher, in 1983.

The Anglo-West Indian Conservative Society has tried to follow suit, but has not succeeded in the same way as the Anglo-Asian Society in creating more local branches and in attracting more members. Councillor Basil Lewis, who had been elected in 1968 for the Conservative party in Haringey, played an active role in establishing the Anglo-West Indian Conservative Society. The society was formally launched in February 1979 to attract voters for the Conservative party.

The Conservative party launched several local initiatives between 1976 and 1979 to win the support of ethnic minorities, in particular of Asians, whose numbers could be crucial in the marginal constituencies. It also decided not to oppose the Race Relations Bill in 1976 on its passage through parliament. In 1977 the Deputy Leader of the party, William Whitelaw, personally supported the campaign of the Federation of Conservative Students against racialism and reaffirmed that the Conservative party was opposed to the activities of the National Front. The party also joined the Joint Committee Against Racialism (JCAR) formed in the Autumn of 1977. The committee included the Liberal and Labour parties, the Board of Deputies of British Jews, the British Council of Churches, the National Union of Students, the British Youth Council, and many national and regional ethnic minority organizations.

The Labour and Conservative parties each nominated one of the two joint chairs. The Labour party nominated Joan Lester MP and the Conservative party John Moore MP though it was reported that Margaret Thatcher was personally opposed to associating with the far left groups. However, the executive committee of the national union decided to continue the Conservative party participation against the wishes of its leader. This decision was unprecedented. Later on, however, Shelagh Roberts, a prominant Conservative from outside parliament, was appointed as joint chair (Layton-Henry 1978). Some of the Conservative party workers who were keen to participate in such activities said at the time that they wanted to demonstrate to the ethnic minorities that they were against any form of racialism in the society. They were optimistic that such genuine efforts would win ethnic minority support for the Conservatives at the ballot box.

However, their optimism was short-lived. On 30 January 1978, Margaret Thatcher, in an interview with Gordon Burns on Granada's *World in Action* programme, said that people were rather afraid that this country and the British character might be swamped by people with a different culture. She added that the Conservative party should hold out the prospect of an end to immigration except in compassionate cases and argued that the neglect of the immigration issue was driving some people to support the National Front. She implied that she wished to attract to the party voters who had been supporting the National Front. She soon appeared to be successful in doing so. Following the interview opinion polls showed that the Conservative party lead rose by 9 per cent over Labour between January and February 1978. Twenty-one per cent of those interviewed mentioned immigration as one of the two most urgent problems facing the country. Before the 30 January interview only 9 per cent of the sample had mentioned immigration as one of the two most urgent problems facing the country (NOP 1978).

Thatcher's interview was criticized widely by politicians, race relations workers, and ethnic minority organizations – and indeed by some of the Conservative party workers who had made great efforts to attract ethnic minorities to the party. As one of them put it at the time,

'she has done considerable damage to our efforts for the time being. Nevertheless, we must carry on to win the confidence and trust of the ethnic minority people as a party. People must be told that Mrs Thatcher was expressing her personal view and that the party policies are clear on race relations and we will eventually win, as a party, the ethnic minority vote.'

There was a lot of activity after this event within the Anglo-Asian Conservative Society to try to reassure its members and other Asians about the good intentions of the Conservative party. They were conscious of the importance of Asian and other ethnic minority votes in over 40 marginal constituencies.

Conservative Central Office and society officials worked actively to arrange meetings between Conservative candidates and ethnic minority groups in the run-up to the 1979 general election. The same pattern of activity applied to the 1983 general election campaign.

The early 1970s saw a trend to the left in the Labour party both on the National Executive and in constituency parties (Hatfield 1978). This helped to create a more positive approach to race relations and towards the ethnic minorities generally to attract their support. When Labour came into power in February 1974, Roy Jenkins, the Home Secretary, announced an amnesty in April 1974 for illegal immigrants who were Commonwealth or Pakistan citizens and who were affected by the retrospective operation of the 1971 Immigration Act passed by the Conservative government. In June of the same year Jenkins allowed the admission of husbands and fiancés of women settled in Britain.

In February 1975 the quota for UK passport holders was raised from 3,600 to 5,000 a year and in September of the same year the White Paper, *Racial Discrimination* (Home Office 1975), was published. This White Paper led to the passing of the Race Relations Act 1976 which replaced the Race Relations Act 1968. The Commission for Racial Equality, which replaced the Community Relations Commission and the Race Relations Board, was created under the new act in 1977. Also in 1977 the Labour government published its Green Paper, *British Nationality Law: Discussion of Possible Changes*. This paper contained proposals for reforming the UK citizenship and nationality laws. Later on, the Nationality Act 1981 was passed by the Conservative government and came into operation from January 1983. The Labour party is committed to repealing this act and replacing it with another one (Labour party manifesto 1983).

The CRC report on the October 1974 general election showed that an overwhelming majority of ethnic minorities had voted for the Labour party. It also became apparent that where other parties had made an effort, they were successful in winning ethnic minority support as, for instance, in Rochdale. However, the growing support for the National Front in some traditionally Labour areas was worrying for the party. For example, in the May 1976 local elections a breakaway group from the National Front, called the National Party had won two seats on the Blackburn District Council. As this had happened in a solid Labour area where

Barbara Castle, a member of the NEC, was the MP (now an MEP), the party was moved to act against the growing racialism in such areas. As a consequence, in September 1976, the NEC agreed to launch a campaign jointly with the TUC to educate Labour party members and trade unionists about the evils of racialism and the dangers of neo-fascist groups such as the National Front. At the time some Labour party activists said that this action was taken partly to demonstrate to the ethnic minorities that the party was in earnest about its concern with their rights and defence against the anti-immigrant organizations, and partly also to attract members for the party from the ethnic minority groups at a time when the Conservative party had helped the formation of the Anglo-Asian Conservative Society.

The Labour Party Race Action Group (LPRAG) was set up in 1975 as a pressure group to educate and advise the party on relevant issues. It distributed a leaflet, *Don't Take Black Votes for Granted*, to all Constituency Labour Parties (CLPs) (LPRAG 1979). The leaflet referred to the CRC report of 1975 and suggested ways and means of attracting ethnic minority support in the 1979 general election. The Home Affairs and Organization Committee of the NEC started looking at the issue of the ethnic minority vote and produced a document, *Labour and the Black Electorate*, which was circulated to all CLPs in February 1980. The document states:

> 'we have, so far, failed to convince black people that we deserve their active support. Instead, they have increasingly been organizing politically into self-help and pressure groups largely spurning mainstream party politics. Indeed, many black people, especially the youngest members of the community, are openly suspicious of the party.'

The document made a number of suggestions to the CLPs about the involvement of ethnic minorities in the party and for methods to convince them that the Labour party was relevant to their needs.

The Home Affairs Committee of the Labour Party's NEC, with the help of working parties, suggested policies on immigration and nationality and 'positive action' which were 'radical' in approach, compared with Labour's previous policies. In addition to the national policies, many CLPs had produced their own literature and organized special meetings to attract the ethnic minority electorate. A lot of such activity was noticed in the London area where an increasing number of ethnic minorities were contesting local elections on the Labour party ticket. Some got elected. The concentration of ethnic minorities in London is crucial for the

Labour party. For example, in 1983, the Inner London Labour-held constituencies had an average of just under 25 per cent of ethnic minority population compared with only half of that figure (12 per cent) in the other Inner London constituencies based on the 1981 census figures. As far as the rest of Greater London was concerned, the Labour-held seats had an average of 22 per cent ethnic minority population compared with 9 per cent in constituencies held by other parties. Therefore, the significance of the ethnic minority vote for the Labour party is obvious.

The Liberal party has been consistently against racial discrimination and discriminatory immigration control (Taylor 1980). The party has always been seen as anti-racist. It opposed the 1968 Commonwealth Immigrants Act passed by the Labour government. It strongly opposed the present government's Nationality Bill and published a document, *A Liberal Nationality Law*, in January 1981 (Liberal party 1981a). The party published a report in September 1981 on *Inner City Disturbances* which was commissioned by the party Leader David Steel. This document critically reviewed the policies of successive governments in the area of race relations, racial disadvantage and related matters.

'If measures to deal with racial disadvantage are taken as one of the tests of political will to deal with urban deprivation, then the record since 1968 can only be regarded as deplorable. In this area of public policy successive governments have been guilty of acts of omission and commission. Among the acts of commission, Mrs Thatcher's pre-election *Granada* interview in which she played the racial card may perhaps be seen as the most flagrant. The Commonwealth Immigrants Act (1968), the Immigration Act (1971) and the Nationality Bill (1981) can all be seen as measures designed to keep out coloured immigrants rather than to control immigration more generally. The Race Relations Act (1968) which was intended to provide a spring-board from which positive policies to tackle racial disadvantage could be launched was interpreted by the then Labour Government as measures that fulfilled their obligations to deal with the problems of the ethnic minorities. Far from being the beginning of a programme to improve race relations in this country, it proved to be the end of their commitment in this field. No effort, for example, was made by successive governments to use Government contracts to ensure equality of opportunities of employment. The Home Office refused to carry out its obligation to co-ordinate government policy, the ethnic question was removed from the census, removing thereby the possibility of monitoring the effectiveness of government policies designed to ensure equality of opportunity.'

(Liberal party 1981b)

This long quote from the Liberal party document highlights Liberal policy in several relevant areas. The 1979 and 1983 general election manifestos confirmed the party's policies and also its views on nationality. For example, *The Liberal Programme* (1982) referred to above sets out the party position on both nationality and race relations. There seemed to be support for such policies among Liberal supporters. The British Election Study of 1974 showed that 42 per cent of 'stalwart Liberals' agreed with the statement that attempts to ensure equality for coloured people in Britain have not gone far enough compared with 23 per cent of supporters of the Conservative and Labour parties (Crewe and Sarlvik 1977).

The Liberal party has a Community Relations Policy Panel, which was until recently chaired by Lord Avebury,[2] a well-known campaigner for the causes of ethnic minorities. This panel meets regularly and gives advice to the party on race and immigration matters; it also helps the party in relevant campaigns and at elections. In 1980 Lord Avebury wrote to all local party chairmen to find out what efforts they were making to recruit ethnic minority people on to their executive committees and to adopt ethnic minority candidates. The party was very active in the JCAR referred to above.

As far as the efforts of the Liberal party to create direct contacts with the ethnic minorities are concerned, a lot of efforts are made locally and Liberal party activists are regularly to be seen at ethnic minority functions. At the national level, in 1982 the party launched a special campaign to attract ethnic minority support. It arranged a press briefing for the ethnic minority press at the House of Commons. Ethnic minority organizations and relevant constituency associations in certain areas were sent policy statements and other literature in the effort to win ethnic minority support for the party in the next general election. How far the party has succeeded in getting that support at the ballot box has been reported in the previous chapter. It would seem, however, that a lot of Asians were sympathetic to the Liberal party but probably did not vote for its candidates where there was no prospect of their winning. Where the Liberal party (and now the Alliance) candidates do stand a chance of winning, ethnic minority electors tend to vote for them. Furthermore, it appears that Liberal candidates attract relatively more 'personal votes' from Asians, in particular, as a result of their regular contact with them.[3] The party leader, David Steel, was reported as saying that the Liberal party has always heralded its commitment to the principles of racial equality of opportunity but attracting members of the black community had never been successful. He declared at a meeting at the House of Commons that the party 'plans to appoint a commission to report about this "black membership drought"'. He added that the Liberal party would field about 12 black candidates at the next general election. He said his party wanted to involve blacks in mainstream politics (*Caribbean Times*, 9 November 1984).

The SDP is a new party and does not therefore have a long history of involvement with ethnic minorities, but its leaders were very active in the field of race relations when part of the Labour party; Roy Jenkins was the most liberal Home Secretary of the Labour government. He was instrumental in introducing the relatively liberal immigration policies of the Labour government from 1974–77 as mentioned above. He was also responsible for the Race Relations Act 1976. Shirley Williams and David Owen were also known to be committed to the issue of racial equality and good race relations as were its many other members. The SDP set up the Social Democratic Campaign for Racial Justice (SDCRJ) to monitor party policy on race and immigration and to give advice and information to the party generally. The national executive committee of the SDP had two ethnic minority members in 1984, both of them elected in open competition. The constitution of the SDP makes provision for co-options to reflect the membership of the party generally, and as a result of this provision, more ethnic minority members have been co-opted.

There is a mandatory provision in the constitution of the SDP for women to be included on the shortlist of candidates, but no such provision exists for the ethnic minority candidates. However, the SDP has put forward candidates from ethnic minorities in both local and parliamentary elections, as I shall discuss below. As the SDP contested the last general election (1983) with the Liberal party in an Alliance, it is not clear from surveys referred to in the previous chapter what sort of support the SDP got from the ethnic minority electorate. However, the SDP leader, David Owen, pleaded for the political participation of ethnic minorities in 1984. He said that black and Asian people in Britain should play a full and active part in national political parties as the best way of confronting and confounding the racism of the National Front. He added that 'people who were victims of violence and injustice should not seek a dialogue with one party only. All political parties need to demonstrate publicly their concern about the growth of racial prejudice' (*Guardian*, 30 April 1984).

On another occasion in 1982 David Owen, speaking to an SDP consultative assembly fringe meeting at Derby, had said that the Social Democrats would have to go for the ethnic minority vote if the Alliance was to stand any chance of winning the next general election (in 1983). He added, 'at the moment, their loyalties are firmly with the Labour party. In the inner cities, the Labour party is getting a very strong automatic vote, still. It can easily shift. Our philosophy is a natural one for many of the ethnic minorities. We have got to get after their attitudes and their thoughts, and then we will get the votes (*The Times*, 14 October 1982). Some considerable efforts were made by the SDP workers to get the ethnic minority support during the 1983 general election.

More recently SDP has published a discussion paper, *Racial Justice* (August 1985), in which key measures have been outlined to end racial injustice. It proposes a human rights commission working directly under a cabinet committee headed by the Home Secretary. The other recommendations in the paper include:

- a government-funded legal advice system for victims of racial harassment;
- positive action to deal with racial disadvantage in jobs, housing and education;
- withdrawal from approved lists of public sector contractors which refuse to operate effective equal opportunities policies.

The paper calls for setting up of 'black enterprise trusts' to give soft loans to ethnic minority entrepreneurs coupled with pre-loan consultancy and after-loan advice. It also draws attention to 'the Labour party's successes in wooing black voters. The London Labour party, and particularly the Labour group on the Greater London Council, have taken great care to solicit the black vote, for example by setting up special ethnic minorities bodies. These tactics "reinforce the impression already prevalent among black voters that the only party interested in black minorities is Labour" and foster a network of groups dependent on the Labour party for financial support "which, then serve as channels for Labour propaganda"' (*Financial Times*, 29 August 1985).

David Owen, SDP leader and Shirley Williams, party president, endorsed the proposals when launching the paper and it is to be debated at the 1985 annual party conference with the view to make it party policy for the next general election. The SDP leadership is aware of the need to involve more people from ethnic minorities in its limits.

'Mrs Williams made it clear that as far as the SDP was concerned there would be no limits for blacks. She said "only on the day when it becomes possible to accept that there is a black or Asian Prime Minister in this country would we be truly committed to race relations".'

'Both she and Dr Owen are opposed to a separate black section in the party and are working towards "colour blind" sections. But both recognise the need to compile a list of party members to ensure they are given adequate representation.'

(*Daily Telegraph*, 29 August 1985)

Now that we have reviewed the efforts of political parties to attract ethnic minority support, let us look at some survey material dealing with the question of ethnic minority participation in mainstream politics and the main political parties. The information relates to both electors and candidates who contested the 1979 and 1983 general elections for the main political parties.

The respondents in the 1974 (CRC) and 1979 (CRE) surveys were asked whether ethnic minority participation in elections should be encouraged.

Seventy-eight per cent of Afro-Caribbeans and 71 per cent of Asians in the 1979 survey said 'yes, it should be encouraged'. At the same time, 58 per cent of whites interviewed in the survey agreed that ethnic minority participation in politics should be encouraged. However, 32 per cent of the white respondents were opposed to their participation as were 6 per cent of Asians and 5 per cent Afro-Caribbeans. *Table 35* gives the details.

More white people intending to vote Conservative were opposed to the participation of ethnic minorities in politics (42 per cent) than were those intending to vote Labour (24 per cent). Conservative candidates,

Table 35 *Ethnic minority participation in politics – electors' views – 1979 survey*

	Total (1,138) %	White (852) %	Afro-Car. (144) %	Asian (397) %
Yes, should be encouraged	65	58	78	71
No, should not	19	32	5	6
Unsure	16	10	17	23

on the other hand, in line with other main party candidates, were generally in favour of encouraging ethnic minorities to participate in politics. Only 6 per cent of Conservative candidates and 2 per cent of Liberal candidates thought that they should not be encouraged to participate. No Labour candidate was of this opinion. On the other hand, 83 per cent of Conservatives, 98 per cent Labour, and 92 per cent Liberals were in favour of the view that ethnic minorities should be encouraged to participate in British politics (see *Table 36*).

If ethnic minorities should be encouraged to participate in politics, what form should their participation take? How can this be achieved? The 1979 results showed that 22 per cent of electors felt that ethnic minority groups should be represented by having politicians in the three main political parties. Almost as many (21 per cent) thought that they should be encouraged to participate in all aspects of political life, while 12 per cent suggested that ethnic minorities should be involved at local level. Thirteen per cent of respondents did not specify the form of participation which they had in mind but felt that ethnic minorities should have a say in the running of the country since they live here.

Those who were opposed to ethnic minority participation in politics were asked the reasons for their view. Seventeen per cent felt that members of ethnic minority groups were unable to understand the problems of British people, British customs and politics. Sixteen per cent replied that 'Britain should be governed by the British/by white people', and a further 12 per cent felt that encouraging participation would lead to ethnic minorities 'taking over' in politics. Nine per cent of respondents put their case even more strongly by saying that ethnic minorities had 'no right' to say how Britain should be governed.

Which political party did they feel was most likely to encourage ethnic minorities to participate in the political process? Thirty-seven per cent of electors felt that the Labour party was most likely to do so. White people

Table 36 *Ethnic minority participation in politics – candidates' views – 1979 survey*

	Total (542) %	Con. (219) %	Lab. (107) %	Lib. (216) %
Yes, should be encouraged	89	83	98	92
No, should not	3	6	—	2
Unsure	8	11	2	6

were marginally more likely (7 per cent) to think the Conservatives were encouraging participation than were either Afro-Caribbean (1 per cent) or Asians (4 per cent). Fourteen per cent thought there was no party which was encouraging participation. It is interesting to see that of those white people who intended to vote Conservative, only 14 per cent thought the Conservatives were actually taking steps to encourage ethnic minority groups, while many more (31 per cent) considered Labour to be doing so. This suggested that many white Conservative supporters were not aware of the efforts that the Conservative party was making to encourage ethnic minority participation in politics.

When questioned about the various ways by which the influence of ethnic minority groups on British politics might be increased, the majority (58 per cent) of respondents were of the view that minority groups should get more involved in the present set-up rather than create their own political parties (14 per cent). Indeed, Afro-Caribbeans were particularly enthusiastic (71 per cent) about minority groups involving themselves in the present set-up, while 60 per cent of Asians interviewed were also of this opinion. Only under 11 per cent of ethnic minority respondents suggested that they should have their own party and over 20 per cent did not have an opinion on this matter.

When we compare these findings with the 1974 survey, we can see that opinion had increased slightly in favour of ethnic minorities participating in the activities of existing political parties. In 1974, 48 per cent of respondents were in favour of this idea compared to 58 per cent in 1979. The greatest change of opinion occurred among the white population (16 per cent against an increase of 10 per cent among Afro-Caribbeans and 2 per cent among Asians). This is an encouraging sign.

It is also encouraging that, in the 1979 survey, over three-quarters (77 per cent) of candidates were in favour of ethnic minorities becoming more involved in existing political arrangements. Labour (96 per cent) and Liberal (94 per cent) candidates were slightly more likely to favour their involvement in this way than Conservative candidates (85 per cent), although the support among Conservative candidates compared with the Conservative supporters was overwhelming.

At the 1983 general election, candidates of the main political parties were again asked questions about the participation of ethnic minorities in British politics. Ninety-four per cent of all the candidates who particpated in the survey felt that ethnic minorities ought to be encouraged to take a more active role in British politics. When asked how they should be encouraged to do this, about a fifth (18 per cent) responded in a general way saying they should take a full part in the democratic process and integrate with society generally. Specific ways mentioned were that ethnic minorities should be encouraged to join and be active in political parties (49 per cent) or other organizations (22 per cent). Ten per cent thought that parties should be sensitive to the needs of ethnic minorities and should talk to community leaders. There were few differences in opinion between the different parties' candidates. The most important was the suggestion by Liberal and SDP candidates that proportional representation would help; this was mentioned by 10 per cent of the Alliance candidates. Some candidates made detailed comments on this issue. For example, a Conservative candidate wrote: 'As Conservatives our appeal is a party which encourages individual initiatives, naturally attractive to Asians particularly. We must talk to Asian community leaders to show our policies'. A Labour candidate suggested that they should be 'encouraged to join the local branch of a union'. A typical answer given by many candidates was illustrated by a Liberal party candidate – 'Parties should try harder to get ethnic candidates'. And an SDP candidate suggested that 'inclusion of ethnic minorities on public boards, school governing bodies' should be encouraged by political parties.

Candidates were asked which of two methods of increasing involvement of ethnic minorities in politics they would favour. Almost all (92 per cent) favoured ethnic minorities getting more involved in the present political parties. No-one favoured the idea of ethnic minorities having their own party. When asked whether ethnic minority candidates should be given safe seats at elections, as many candidates overall supported this notion (35 per cent) as were opposed to it (35 per cent). Conservative candidates were more likely to reject the suggestion (58 per cent) than candidates from other parties (Labour 22 per cent, Liberals 29 per cent, and SDP 31 per cent).

Ethnic minority candidates

One way to look at the response of the political parties and to examine the integration of ethnic minorities into the political process is to look at the number of candidates adopted by the main political parties in the last few years. It is by incorporating ethnic minorities into the political system, not as nominal, but as effective members who participate actively in the decision-making process, that their alienation can be prevented. Looking at the American experience, we find that the number of blacks registered to vote in the 11 southern states increased between 1962 and 1974 from $1\frac{1}{2}$ million to $3\frac{1}{2}$ million (though there were two million eligible black voters still unregistered). That vote was reflected in their representation. By 1974 in the whole of the United States black representation was: one black senator, 16 members of the House of Representatives, and 108 mayors. For the first time in the history of the US, apart from the brief, false dawn after the Civil War, blacks had been incorporated into the American political system and their political aspirations had a legitimate and constitutional means of expression. No doubt the psychological effect of this revolution was as important as the strictly political (Bonham-Carter 1979). More recently, one of the 1984 presidential candidates, the Reverend Jesse Jackson, made this effect even greater when as a black American he sought presidential nomination for the Democratic party, and reached the last three of the Democratic party contenders. His contest was seen as a boost to the political participation of blacks in America. Jackson's campaign helped to increased registration among black Americans and gave considerable strength to the demands for blacks to seek a greater share of political offices. His campaign was also seen by many blacks in Britain as an encouragement for them to press for greater representation in this country.

General elections

While there have been no MPs from the ethnic minority groups since the Second World War, a number of parliamentary candidates have been members of these groups. The first was Sardar K. S. N. Ahluwala who stood in Willesden West for the Liberal party in 1950. He polled 2,853 votes, which was just over 5 per cent of the total votes cast in this constituency. But the most notable of the ethnic minority candidates was David Thomas Pitt (now Lord) who contested Hampstead in 1959 and Clapham in 1970 for the Labour party. In the general election of 1959 he received 13,500 votes, 28.3 per cent of the total votes cast in the Hampstead constituency. The loss of votes was 3.5 per cent in this constituency compared with a national swing of 2.6 per cent against Labour in this election. For Dr Pitt's 1970 result, see below, p. 99.

In the 1964 general election no ethnic minority candidates stood on behalf of the main political parties. However, there was an Independent candidate, A. B. Abbas, who stood in Holborn and St Pancras South. He received only 226 votes, 0.8 per cent of the total votes cast in this constituency.

In the general election in 1970 there were eight ethnic minority candidates. These included one for Labour, David Pitt (Clapham), three Liberals, Preetam Singh (Sheffield Hallam), Mihir Gupta (Smethwick), and Ghulam Musa (Bradford East); three Independents, A. Qureshi (Hackney Central), Dhram Das (Wolverhampton South-West), and Tonderai Makoni (Howden); Saeed-uz-Zafar stood as British Commonwealth candidate. None of these was elected, but David Pitt's defeat surprised the Labour party. He was contesting a reasonably safe Labour seat. David Pitt was defeated with a 10.2 per cent swing from Labour to Conservative, over twice the swing in the surrounding constituencies. The Labour vote was down (11.2 per cent) compared with the national loss of 4.9 per cent and the total turnout was down (11 per cent). The conclusion seems inescapable that some Labour voters did not vote because their candidate was black (Spencer 1970: 260–67). The Labour vote of 19,555 in 1966 was down to 13,473 in 1970 and the Conservatives won the seat with a majority of 3,120 (Anwar and Kohler 1975).

In David Pitt's case, even if one takes into account local circumstances – he was nominated for this constituency only three weeks before the election, he faced a locally well-known Conservative, and he did not himself live in the constituency – it is difficult to explain in any other way other than his colour the degree of his rejection by Labour voters (Deakin and Bourne 1970). No other ethnic minority candidate received more than 7.3 per cent of the vote.

In the February 1974 general election the Labour party put forward a Pakistani, councillor Bashir Maan from Glasgow, to contest East Fife. There were five other ethnic minority candidates in this election: Dhani Prem (Coventry South-East) standing for the Liberals; Baldev Singh Chahal (Southall Ealing) Anti-Helmet candidate; Tariq Ali (Sheffield Attercliffe) International Marxist Group; Sylvester Smart (Lambeth Central) Workers Revolutionary Party; and Ekins Brome (Lambeth Central) for the Communist Party of England (Marxist-Leninist). The Liberal Candidate Dhani Prem received 4,472 votes, which was 11.7 per cent of the total votes cast in his constituency. The four other fringe party candidates together received only 1,178 votes. The Labour candidate Bashir Maan, however, got 6,634 votes, 15 per cent of the total votes cast, which was a reduction of the Labour share in this constituency. See *Table 37* for details.

It appeared that Maan, like other ethnic minority candidates up to that time, suffered because of his colour. While there were other factors at the time to be taken into account, for example, the strong advance of the

Table 37 *East Fife constituency results of the general elections, 1970, February 1974, and October 1974*

	1970	Feb. 1974	Oct. 1974
Conservative	21,619	21,172	16,116
Labour	9,756	6,634	7,040
Scottish Nationalist	4,666	8,593	13,202
Liberal	3,577	7,766	5,247

Scottish Nationalists, the advance of the Liberal party in February 1974, and a minor revision of the constituency between 1970 and February 1974, it would nevertheless appear that a proportion of Labour supporters who might have voted for a white candidate did not vote for Bashir Maan.

In the October 1974 general election there were three ethnic minority candidates, of whom only one, Cecil Williams (Liberal), stood for one of the main political parties. He contested Birmingham, Sparkbrook. The other two candidates were Sylvester Smart (Lambeth Central), Workers Revolutionary Party, who also stood in the February election, and Chandra Rao (Hampstead), an Independent candidate. Among these Smart and Rao received only 233 and 31 votes respectively. However, Williams (Liberal) received 2,921 votes, 9.8 per cent of the total votes cast in the Sparkbrook constituency. In September 1974 he had received 15.8 per cent of the votes in a council by-election in the Sparkbrook ward.

Before we look at the ethnic minority candidates in the 1979 and 1983 general elections and two by-elections in 1977 and 1979 in which ethnic minority candidates had contested, it is relevant to report here the results of a survey undertaken on the subject of ethnic minority candidates just before the October 1974 general election. These results should help to detect the existence of prejudice among electors against ethnic minority candidates at that time (over 10 years ago). Respondents were asked how likely they were to vote for the party they had said they would support. Later in the questionnaire the same question was asked with the addition of 'if the candidate were West Indian or Asian'. By comparing the replies to the question we can discover the effect of having an ethnic minority candidate. The results are given in *Table 38*.

Although some of the samples were small and should be treated with caution, it is clear that a substantial proportion of white voters for all

Table 38 *Likelihood to vote: 1974 Survey*

1. *How likely is it that you will vote for the ... (party supported at previous election) candidate in this constituency in the general election?*

	Labour		Conservative		Liberal	
	White (159) %	Ethnic minority (191) %	White (88) %	Ethnic minority (29) %	White (49) %	Ethnic minority (18) %
'Extremely likely' or 'very likely'	80	79	81	69	77	72

2. *How likely would you be to vote for the ... candidate (party supported at previous question) at the general election if he were West Indian or Asian?*

	Labour		Conservative		Liberal	
	White %	Ethnic minority %	White %	Ethnic minority %	White %	Ethnic minority %
'Extremely likely' or 'very likely'	59	75	49	66	57	72

three parties were less likely to vote for an ethnic minority candidate. One in four Labour voters were no longer determined to vote if the candidate was West Indian or Asian – and three out of eight Conservatives. This confirms the handicap for an ethnic minority candidate, but also shows it is not insuperable if the constituency is sufficiently 'safe' (Anwar and Kohler 1975). But the results of further surveys in 1979 and 1983 show that this handicap is disappearing (see below) and that both whites and ethnic minorities vote on party lines, not on an ethnic basis.

In the Ladywood (Birmingham) by-election in August 1977 three ethnic minority candidates stood: R. Ahsan (Socialist Unity), K. Gordon (Socialist Workers Party), and J. Hunte (Independent). They polled 336, 534, and 152 votes respectively, together making 6.6 per cent of the total votes cast and accounting for 'probably' 12 per cent of the ethnic minority vote (Layton-Henry and Taylor 1978). It appeared that ethnic minority voters, who constituted about 40 per cent of the electorate, voted overwhelmingly for the Labour party candidate. Thus the disproportionate number of Labour votes among ethnic minority electors contributed substantially to Labour's margin of victory (Layton-Henry and Taylor 1977). It was observed, based on this trend, that the Labour candidate would have won without the ethnic minority vote, but only just. However, if a block of ethnic minority voters had voted for the other candidates, Labour could have lost the seat. In April 1978 one ethnic minority candidate, J. A. Chase (Socialist Unity), contested the Lambeth Central by-election. He received only 287 votes, which was 1.4 per cent of the total votes cast.

Because of the importance of the ethnic minority vote, and to repair the damaged image of the Conservative party with the ethnic minorities, the Tories launched an advertising campaign in September 1978. It was reported by the *Sunday Telegraph* – 'How Tories are wooing immigrants' (*Sunday Telegraph*, 24 September 1978) – and by the *Financial Times*: 'Immigrant vote drive launched by Tories' (*Financial Times*, 18 September 1978). It was claimed at the time by some Conservative party workers that this campaign had a good effect. They also claimed that, in spite of the Conservative party image regarding the immigration policy, many Asians had voted for the Conservative candidate in the Ilford North by-election earlier that year, when it was reported that the ethnic minority vote was crucial: 'Immigrants hold key in changing face of by-election' (*Guardian*, 15 March 1978); and *The Times* reported 'Ilford: which way will the Asians vote?' (*The Times*, 21 February 1978). The Conservative party workers also hoped that in the next general election (1979) many ethnic minorities would vote Tory.

Of the 12 ethnic minority candidates in the 1979 general election, five were put forward by the three main political parties. This was the first time since 1945 that the Conservative party had nominated ethnic minority candidates. The ethnic minority candidates standing for the three main political parties were:

Name of candidate	Constituency	Party
Farooq Saleem	Glasgow Central	Conservative
Narindar Saroop	Greenwich	Conservative
Russell Profitt	Westminster South	Labour
Cecil Williams	Nuneaton	Liberal
Raj-Mal Singh	Coventry, N.E.	Liberal

In the event, none of these was elected. How did they 'perform' as candidates and how did their party performance in 1974 compare with that of

ethnic minority candidates in 1979? Our analysis showed that the two
Conservative candidates, in line with the general trend, actually improved
their party's vote in their respective constituencies. The one Labour
candidate also performed as well as the national trend for Labour might
have suggested; but the two Liberal candidates did badly (*Table 39*
presents the details). This could have had something to do with, among
other things, the nationwide reduction in the Liberal share of the vote
which occured in 1979 compared with the 1974 elections. Another
reason could have been the fact that Raj-Mal Singh in Coventry North-
East was adopted by the Liberals just before the 1979 election and Cecil
Williams received a divided Liberal support when he was adopted in
Nuneaton (*The Times*, 18 April 1978).

The other ethnic minority candidates included: H. Harewood
(Lewisham East), G. Dacres (Lewisham Deptford), and O. Banjo (City of
Westminster and Paddington), all standing for the Workers' Revolutionary Party and none winning more than 198 votes; T. Ali (Ealing Southall)
representing the Socialist Unity Party polled 477 votes; J. N. Bardway
(Luton East) for the Committee for Prevention of Police State received 61
votes; S. Gupta (Ealing Southall) as an Independent and S. S. Paul
(Ealing Southall) as an Independent Businessman received 637 and 115
votes respectively. In a Manchester Central by-election later in September
1979 an Independent Labour candidate, Syed Ala-Ud-Din, received 187
votes. He had declared at the time that he was standing as a protest

Table 39 *Share of votes received by ethnic minority candidates in 1979 and
previous electoral performance of that party*

Candidate	Constituency	Party share in		
		May 1979	October 1974	February 1974
Farooq Saleem (Con.)	Glasgow Central	1,934 (16.4%)	1,880 (13%)	3,435 (21.4%)
Narindar Saroop (Con.)	Greenwich	12,133 (33.3%)	9,249 (26.8%)	11,294 (28.7%)
Russell Profitt (Lab.)	City of London Westminster South	7,067 (25.4%)	8,589 (30.9%)	8,698 (27.3%)
Raj-Mal Singh (Lib.)	Coventry North-East	2,291 (4.9%)	6,846 (15.4%)	—
Cecil Williams (Lib.)	Nuneaton	6,184 (9.8%)	10,729 (18.6%)	12,591 (19.8%)

against the Labour party which had refused to adopt him as its candidate in that election. This by-election was won by the Labour candidate.

Syed Ala-Ud-Din's protest, however, raised an important question about the adoption of ethnic minority candidates and the frustration of those who feel that they are not getting 'safe' or 'winnable' seats. The recent debate about the demand for black sections within the Labour party, it seems, is centred partly around this issue. Many ethnic minority candidates and potential candidates have expressed their dissatisfaction about the main political parties' attitudes to giving ethnic minority candidates 'safe' seats. They feel 'parties are not serious', 'it is all tokenism' and so on.

Some ethnic minority candidates complained that they did not get the type of support at the election provided for white candidates by the party machinery. For example, at least two candidates who were standing in 1979 for the main political parties told the author that they did not get the campaign material on time. One of them said 'White party workers did not care and some said why work too hard? We are not going to win this seat.' Are ethnic minority candidates' complaints about the indifferent attitudes of the political parties' machinery justified? There is no way to check this but, if ethnic minority candidates feel this way, the implication is that they were probably not being accepted as 'serious' candidates.

At the 1983 general election 18 ethnic minority candidates were selected to stand for the major (four) political parties, compared with only five candidates in 1979. *Table 40* gives the name, party, constituency, NWCP population in 1981, and votes received in the election. As we know, none of them was elected. It is worth emphasizing that none of these 18 got a safe seat and only one of them, Paul Boateng (Labour) in Hertfordshire West, was contesting a marginally winnable seat. However, there was a lot of pre-election interest in the potential performance of these candidates, as there was in the ethnic minority vote. One paper reported on 'The blacks most likely to get to Westminster', giving a brief profile of some ethnic minority candidates who were already selected for the 1983 general election (*The Times*, 18 March 1983). On 11 March 1983 several papers carried stories about the Asian candidate for Birmingham Ladywood, Pramila LeHunte, chosen by the Conservative party (*Daily Telegraph, The Times, Guardian*, and other daily papers). Later, on 30 March 1983, the *Daily Telegraph* ran a profile of LeHunte with her picture saying that she hoped to become Britain's first woman ethnic minority MP. There were several other articles in the press about the

Table 40 *Ethnic minority candidates: 1983 general election*

Candidate	Party	Constituency	NCWP population in 1981 % of total	Votes received
H. Gardener	Con.	Newham North-East	32.6	10,773
P. LeHunte	Con.	Birmingham Ladywood	42.0	10,248
P. Nischal	Con.	Birmingham Small Heath	36.0	7,262
S. Popat	Con.	North Durham	0.3	12,418
P. Boateng	Lab.	Herts. West	2.5	13,045
B. Bousquet	Lab.	Kensington	11.0	9,173
R. Austin	Lab.	St Albans	3.5	6,213
D. Colin Thome	Lab.	Warrington South	1.0	16,275
J. Thakoordin	Lab.	Milton Keynes	4.0	13,045
K. Vaz	Lab.	Richmond and Barnes	4.0	3,126
A. Alagappa	Lib.	Feltham and Heston	19.6	8,706
Z. Gifford	Lib.	Hertsmere	2.5	13,758
M. Nadeem	Lib.	Ealing Southall	43.7	8,059
G. Williams	Lib.	Birmingham Perry Barr	16.0	4,773
A. Ahmed	SDP	Manchester Central	9.0	4,956
S. Fernando	SDP	Leicester West	12.0	5,935
T. Mann	SDP	Brent North	24.0	9,082
O. Parmar	SDP	Birmingham Sparkbrook	36.0	4,956

ethnic minority candidates. One reason for all this publicity was to attract ethnic minority votes, not only for these candidates, but also for other candidates from their parties, particularly in areas where the ethnic minority vote held the key.

In addition to the 18 ethnic minority candidates who stood for the main political parties (Conservative [4], Labour [6], Liberal [4], and SDP [4]), there were another seven who stood as Independent or fringe party candidates. None of these seven received more than 970 votes and the lowest of them received only 54 votes.

Post-election analyses of the performance of the ethnic minority candidates reached varying conclusions. Some argued that these candidates faced discrimination by white voters; others suggested that their performance was better than the previous results for the same party (Le Lohe 1983; FitzGerald 1983). However, what is lacking in these analyses is the actual voting patterns of whites and ethnic minorities in the constituencies with an ethnic minority candidate. In the CRE's survey of

1983 we obtained this evidence by covering five constituencies with an ethnic minority candidate standing for the four main political parties. See *Table 41*.

It is difficult to isolate the impact that an ethnic minority candidate has in an individual constituency without taking into account national trends and local factors. The exit poll data, however, is unique in that it provides voting patterns broken down by race and so one can compare the relative share of the vote gained by each candidate amongst white and ethnic minority voters.

Table 41 shows that in two of the five constituencies with an ethnic minority candidate, the white vote percentage was higher than the ethnic vote percentage for the ethnic minority candidate, irrespective of which party was represented. In two other constituencies, the base number of whites (Ealing Southall) and ethnic minorities (Hertfordshire West) were very low indeed, thus preventing any firm conclusions. However, in Ealing Southall an overwhelming majority of ethnic minorities voted for the white Labour party candidate and not for the Asian candidate who was contesting this seat for the Alliance. In Manchester Central, a Labour stronghold, the ethnic minority vote percentage was higher than the white vote percentage both for the white Labour candidate and for the ethnic minority candidate standing for the Alliance. These results suggest that party allegiances are more important in determining the outcome of the result than the race of the candidate.

These results are quite different from the results mentioned above for the early 1970s. This also means that if ethnic minority candidates are adopted in 'safe' seats they are as likely to win as any other candidates. There is also evidence that these constituencies need not be ones with a higher concentration of ethnic minority electors. Even following Mich Le Lohe's analysis, the evidence from the 1983 general election was that, even with the exception of about 10 per cent of the constituencies where an ethnic minority candidate might lose because of discrimination by white voters, there is nothing to suggest that an ethnic minority candidate will lose the seat (Le Lohe 1983).

The situation in terms of accepting ethnic minority candidates as 'party candidates' seems quite different from what we discovered in 1974. In general, most of the ethnic minority candidates in 1983 who stood for the main political parties performed like any other candidate for their respective parties. For example, in 17 of the 18 constituencies contested, where comparison with the notional party position in 1979 was possible, the parties' position was unchanged. It was Paul Boateng (Labour) in

Table 41 *Some constituencies with ethnic minority candidates standing for major parties – voting patterns by ethnic groups*

	White	All ethnic minorities
Birmingham Ladywood – Conservative candidate		
	(54)	*(108)*
Base	%	%
Labour	64	79
Conservative	29	6
Alliance	5	11
Other	2	4
Birmingham Sparkbrook – Alliance (SDP) candidate		
	(44)	*(90)*
Base	%	%
Labour	44	83
Conservative	22	12
Alliance	13	3
Other	22	5
Ealing Southall – Alliance (Liberal) candidate		
	(2)	*(162)*
Base	No.	%
Labour	—	86
Conservative	(2)	—
Alliance	—	13
Other	—	1
Herfordshire West – Labour candidate		
	(168)	*(6)*
Base	%	No.
Conservative	47	(1)
Labour	20	(3)
Alliance	32	(2)
Other	—	—
Manchester Central – Alliance (SDP) candidate		
	(84)	*(79)*
Base	%	%
Labour	78	81
Conservative	17	3
Alliance	5	16
Other	—	—

Note: ( ) = small bases: percentages are meaningless so the actual figures are included for information only.

Hertfordshire West who was relegated to third position in this election while in 1979 the Labour party had won this seat. Yet he was the only ethnic minority candidate who had a chance of winning. However, we know that his adoption as a Labour candidate received divided support and a lot of bad publicity in the media which probably did not help. There seemed to be other factors.

Why were there so many Independent and fringe party ethnic minority candidates in these elections? For example, between the 1950 and 1979 general elections altogether 37 ethnic minority candidates stood and out of these 23 were Independent or fringe party candidates. The 1983 general election was the first time that the number of those standing for the main political parties was greater (18) than the Independent and fringe party candidates (7). However, of a total of 62 ethnic minority candidates in general elections and parliamentary by-elections since 1950, 30 belonged to Independent and fringe parties. Their performance in these elections was 'poor' compared with those who stood for the main political parties. But why did these candidates stand in those elections? Some, like other fringe or Independent candidates in elections, stood because they wanted to air some issue(s), others stood for small parties, and still others stood because they wanted to protest against the lack of ethnic minority representation in the House of Commons.

It was clear that they were not hoping to win but to 'make a point'. Sometimes the intervention of these independent candidates can upset the balance in a contest and hence change the result in a marginal constituency. For example, in the 1983 general election, it is assumed that R. Ganatra (Independent) in Leicester East, who received 970 votes, the highest among the ethnic minority candidates standing as Independents or for fringe parties, cost the Labour party this seat, because the Conservative candidate, Peter Bruinvels, won the seat by only 933 votes. Patricia Hewitt (Labour) was quoted before the election as saying that she was worried that the party vote could be split by the Asian Independent candidate, R. Ganatra, and the sitting SDP MP, T. Bradley. She said, 'We cannot take the ethnic vote for granted' (*Observer*, 22 May 1983). At the 1979 general election Bradley had been elected for Labour with a majority of 2,856. Ganatra, however, seemed a serious threat to a united Asian vote. 'Spurning party labels, he bases his appeal on the need for the Asians to have one of their own community in parliament' (*Observer*, 22 May 1983). In addition to this factor it appeared that the Conservative candidate had also won some support from Asians in this constituency. However, the main point to be made here is that Independent or fringe party ethnic minority candidates do badly because an overwhelming majority of ethnic minorities vote on party lines, not for individuals.

Local elections

The performance of ethnic minority candidates has been relatively better in local than in parliamentary elections. For example, Lord Pitt had been the Labour representative on the GLC for North Hackney and Stoke Newington, which had the same boundaries as the parliamentary constituency. He became the first ethnic minority chair of the GLC in 1974–5. More recently in 1981 Paul Boateng (Labour) was elected to the GLC and became the chair of its Police Committee.

Similarly, other candidates from ethnic minority communities have been elected to local councils but it is not possible to present a full picture of the total number of ethnic minority candidates and their successes or failures in the last two decades. However, a few examples over time will be presented to make some relevant points. In the London Borough elections in May 1974, 12 ethnic minority councillors were elected, 10 for Labour and two for the Conservatives. In 1978, 35 ethnic minority candidates were elected. These included 29 Labour, five Conservatives, and one Independent, Gupta in the Northcote ward of Ealing.

By 1982 this number had risen to 79 in the London Borough elections, in which a total number of 1,914 councillors were elected. Sixty-nine of these were elected for Labour, seven for the Conservatives, two for the Liberals, and one as an Independent. Forty-two were Asians and 37 Afro-Caribbeans. It is estimated that the total number of ethnic minority candidates in this election in London boroughs was 250. Out of these, almost 100 were selected by the Labour party, about 45 by the Conservative party, 50 by the SDP, and 30 by the Liberals. Others were standing either as Independent or for the fringe parties. This number is no doubt an increase upon previous election figures in 1978 for ethnic minority candidates but certainly not sufficient to warrant equal opportunity for ethnic minorities in the local decision-making process. For example, the total number of candidates in London Borough elections was 5,992, and 5,579 of these stood for the four main political parties.

Out of these, an estimated 225 ethnic minority candidates, only 4 per cent of the total, stood for the main political parties. The number of elected ethnic minority councillors is also 4 per cent of the total in the 32 London boroughs. However, the overall ethnic minority population in these boroughs was over 12 per cent. Therefore, the political parties need to go a long way to achieve any realistic representation of ethnic minorities at the local level. Generally, the success rate of the ethnic minority candidates standing for the Labour party was much better (over 60 per cent) than for those standing for other parties.

Outside London the situation of ethnic minority candidates and elected councillors was worse. For example, in the April and May 1973 elections, County and District Council respectively, only six ethnic minority candidates were elected. With the exception of one Liberal in Rochdale, all others belonged to the Labour party. Many other ethnic minority candidates were unsuccessful at local elections.

Mich Le Lohe of Bradford University has monitored local elections in relation to ethnic minority participation since the early 1960s, particularly in Bradford. He also undertook some work in this connection that was funded by the CRE specifically to look at the County Council elections in 1981 and District Council elections in 1982 (Le Lohe 1982). Here some of that analysis is used. In the 1977 County Council elections there were 37 ethnic minority candidates, 17 Labour, 11 Liberal, 2 Conservative, 2 Communist, one Asian Socialist League, and 4 Independent. Of these, four were elected: three Labour, one in each of the counties of West Yorkshire, Leicestershire, and Warwickshire, and one Conservative in Cambridge. The three Labour candidates who were elected were fighting safe Labour seats. Seven ethnic minority candidates were contesting a 'possible' seat including the one Conservative who was elected. The remaining 27 candidates were contesting 'poor seats'.

In the 1981 County Council elections there were 54 ethnic minority candidates, of whom 12 were elected (10 Labour, one Conservative, and one Independent). The party line-up for ethnic minority candidates was as follows: Labour 19, Conservative 10, Liberals 8, Communist 2, Social Democratic 2; the other 13 were standing either as Independents (5) or for other smaller parties. Only four of Labour's ethnic minority candidates were fighting safe seats. The other six who were successful were contesting marginal 'possible' seats. As it was a good year for the Labour party, the six marginals were won. Conversely, it was not a good year for the Conservative party and out of their three best prospects where ethnic minority candidates were standing only one managed to hold on to his seat, in Cambridgeshire.

From the comparison of the 1977 and 1981 County Council elections we can see that although the number of ethnic minority candidates as well as elected councillors had increased in 1981, they still constituted only 0.3 per cent of the total number of almost 4,000 county councillors in England. The Greater London Council had only one ethnic minority councillor out of its 92. Out of the six Metropolitan County Councils of 600 councillors, only one, West Midlands, had an ethnic minority councillor. Greater Manchester, Merseyside, South Yorkshire, West Yorkshire, and Tyne and Wear, with their large concentrations of ethnic minorities, had no councillor from these communities. This situation clearly was not satisfactory.

Let us now look at the District Council elections of 1978, 1979, 1980, and 1982, to see the participation of ethnic minority candidates.[4] In 1978 outside London (for London see above), in the Metropolitan and non-Metropolitan District Council elections there were 23 ethnic minority candidates (the same number as in 1976) out of a total of over 4,000 candidates contesting these elections. Nine of these were Labour, three Conservative, and two Liberals. The remaining nine were standing as Independent or as minor parties' candidates. Out of these only seven Labour candidates and one Independent ethnic minority candidate were elected.

The information about the 1979 and 1980 local elections applies to Asian candidates only because of lack of information about other ethnic minority candidates. Even with Asian names which are anglicized there is a chance of small error. However, one purpose here is to look at general trends and not precise figures.

In 1979 the elections were held in 36 Metropolitan and all the 296 non-Metropolitan districts in England. Three of the Metropolitan and 252 of the non-Metropolitan districts held elections for the whole council and there were normally more than one councillor to be elected in a ward, thus increasing the chances of the adoption of ethnic minority candidates, especially as each of the three main political parties had the opportunity to produce three candidates for one ward instead of just one. In this way, the political parties might 'balance the slate' by having one or more ethnic minority candidates. As Le Lohe put it, 'Thus all parties show some tendency to include some from the ethnic minorities in some of their "slates" particularly when contesting inner urban seats' (Le Lohe 1984). Also the political parties have to find a large number of candidates and the chances of ethnic minorities and of women gaining adoption are considerably increased.

In the 1979 local elections, 58 Asian candidates were identified. Of these 31 were Labour, eight Liberals, seven Conservatives, while twelve stood as Independent or for fringe parties. Seven of these Asian candidates were elected, five Labour, and two Conservatives. This was a very low figure given the large number of seats contested by all the candidates in these elections.

In the 1980 district elections, which took place in 36 Metropolitan districts in England and 103 of the other districts, 32 Asian candidates were identified. Of these, 12 each were standing for the Labour and Conservative parties, three for the Liberal party, and five as Independents and for minor parties. Six of these Asian candidates were elected, five Labour, and one Independent. Three of the Labour victories were in Bradford where for the first time the number of Asian councillors had reached three. The other two Labour victories were in Wolverhampton. The Independent Asian victor was in Hart District Council in Hampshire. Looking at the type of seats given to Asians in this election, the five Labour candidates who were successful all won 'safe' seats while none of the Asian Conservative candidates had any chance of winning.

The 1982 local elections took place in all the Metropolitan districts in England and 102 of the non-Metropolitan and County districts, including London and Scotland. Outside London, 81 ethnic minority candidates were identified in this election. These included: 34 Labour, 20 SDP, nine Conservatives, six Liberals, and another 12 standing as Independents and for fringe parties. Only 12 of these were successful, 10 for the Labour party and two for the SDP, and no ethnic minority candidate standing as Conservative was successful. It appears from all the results that the Labour party is putting forward more ethnic minority candidates for 'winnable' and 'safe' seats compared with the other main political parties. Let us look at some recent local examples.

At the 1982 local elections in Birmingham there were 375 candidates and 23 of these were from ethnic minority communities, with 21 standing for the three main parties. Of these, only five Labour party candidates were elected. In Leicester, in the 1983 local elections, out of 173 candidates, 33 were from ethnic minorities, 27 of these standing for the four main parties. These included 13 for the Alliance, nine for the Labour party, and five for the Conservative party. Eight of the nine Labour candidates were successful while no other ethnic minority candidate got in. Similarly, in a comparatively small place like Luton, there were 13 ethnic minority candidates in 1983. These included seven Labour and two Conservatives. Only three ethnic minority Labour candidates were successful. Slough, in 1983, had 18 ethnic minority candidates including five Labour, two of whom were successful. This pattern seems to be repeated again and again, in particular when we look at some London boroughs. For example, in Brent in 1982, there were 13 ethnic minority councillors. Twelve of these belonged to the Labour party (one later defected to the Conservatives). Ealing had eight ethnic minority councillors, all Labour. Hackney,

Newham, and Waltham Forest had the same sort of pattern as far as ethnic minority representation is concerned.

Another way to check the performance of ethnic minority candidates is to look at their share of vote compared to the white candidates from the same party for multiple vacancies contests. Mich le Lohe (1982) has done such an analysis for local elections. In the 1982 local elections there were 31 comparable contests outside London. These were in Birmingham, Manchester, Dudley, Kirklees, and North Tyneside. On 'party slates' in 21 of the 31 comparable contests ethnic minority candidates ran behind their white colleagues. But in 10 contests they were ahead of their white fellow contestants. In the 13 Labour party instances the average ethnic minority candidate's share was equal to 89.5 per cent of the white candidate's vote, and the latter were ahead in 12 out of 13 contests.

Comparatively the Conservative ethnic minority candidates performed better. In all three instances the ethnic minority Conservative candidates were ahead on the 'slate' with an average vote equal to 106.4 per cent of their white Conservative running mates. With the Liberals and Social Democrats there were six instances out of 15 in which the ethnic minority candidates were ahead of their white colleagues. Their average vote was 100.6 per cent of their white partners.

However, the close examination of the findings show that in addition to the political party for which an ethnic minority candidate is standing it is also relevant to bear in mind the ethnic composition of the area of contest as well as the personal popularity of a candidate both among ethnic minorities and white voters. For example, in the 10 instances in which the ethnic minority candidates received more votes than their white colleagues, six of them (two Conservative, three Alliance, and one Labour) were in the Birmingham wards of Aston, Handsworth, Spark-book, and Sparkhill (see p. 22 for ethnic minority population in these wards). Three of the remaining five were in Manchester wards with ethnic minority concentrations and the last one was in Wakefield, a ward without an ethnic minority concentration where an Asian doctor on average received 157.1 per cent of the vote received by his white Alliance candidate. It was reported that this result was due to his personal popularity. In Southall in three wards with Asian concentrations the average share of Asian Labour candidates ranged between 106.5 and 111.2 per cent of their white colleagues from the same party contesting the same wards.

All these analyses show that the phenomenon of the performance of an ethnic minority candidate is complex. There could be many factors and these could vary according to party label, characteristics of the area of contest, personal popularity of a candidate, rejection by some white voters on grounds of colour, and whether the seat is 'safe' or 'winnable'. Some of these reasons could equally apply to a white candidate. However, there is enough evidence to indicate that in the 1980s, generally, ethnic minority candidates are being accepted as 'party' candidates.

To conclude this section it would be appropriate to mention that the number of ethnic minority candidates, as well as their successes, has been increasing slowly. The political parties have started taking much more interest in putting forward ethnic minority candidates and canvassing for them. For example, in a local council by-election in Bradford in February 1985, for the first time three main political parties put forward Asian candidates. They all came from Pakistan. It was reported in some national newspaper that this contest was making 'political history' (*Daily Mail*, 4 February 1985). The campaign attracted some national political figures who came to Bradford to canvass, particularly for the Conservative candidate. A lot of interest was created during the campaign in which not only the local issues but also the national policies of the political parties were debated in public meetings. *The Jang* (Urdu daily) regularly carried detailed coverage of these meetings. The Labour candidate in this election won the seat but the activities and the attitudes of the political parties showed that they were no longer worried about losing the white electors' support. In 1985, ethnic minority candidates are generally being accepted as 'party candidates' both by whites and by ethnic minority electors, irrespective of their colour, and political parties need not worry about losing white electors' support.

The ethnic minorities' response

Here we discuss various aspects of the ethnic minorities' response to the issue of political participation. The analysis presented in this chapter also includes survey material to illustrate some of the aspects of participation of both ethnic minorities and whites. Let us begin by looking at the membership of political parties and trades unions.

Membership of and participation in political parties

In the 1974 CRC survey, respondents from seven constituencies were asked about their membership of political parties. Only 2 per cent of whites, 3 per cent of Afro-Caribbeans, and less than 1 per cent of Asians reported membership of a political party. They were almost all members of the Labour party. However, membership of trades unions was higher. Almost 22 per cent of whites, 28 per cent of Afro-Caribbeans, and 27 per cent of Asians interviewed claimed that they belonged to trades unions.

In the 1979 survey (Anwar 1980a) respondents were asked about membership of political parties and trades unions. Only 28 per cent belonged to any organization. When this figure was broken down into ethnic origins, it was found that 34 per cent of Afro-Caribbean respondents belonged to some organization, compared with 24 per cent among Asians and 29 per cent among whites. The majority of those who claimed to belong to some organization belonged to a trades union. This level of participation in organizations is very similar to that which was found in the 1974 survey to which we referred above.

The majority of the respondents were unlikely either to belong to a British political party or ever to have attended a party political meeting. Only 17 per cent of the total sample of respondents had ever attended party political meetings and of these, Asians were the least likely to have done so (7 per cent) and Afro-Caribbeans less likely (10 per cent) than white voters who showed a more favourable response (26 per cent).

Looking at the age profiles of those likely to attend these meetings it was found that those who were over 35 years of age among the white sample were more likely to have attended such meetings, while among Afro-Caribbeans it was primarily those under 35 years of age. The Asian sample was too small for such analysis. It must be remembered that only 5 per cent of the adults in the UK were members of political parties (Rose 1980: 178) and the low figures for ethnic minorities in this context are not therefore surprising.[1]

Further evidence about some aspects of the political involvement of ethnic minorities as far as the survey material is concerned can be found in the Gallup election surveys before the 1979 general election (Studlar and Layton-Henry 1984). Ethnic minorities appeared to display a roughly equal amount of interest in the election and its outcome. *Table 42* gives details which illustrate this point. Although the ethnic minority samples are small in comparison with the white samples, the analysis gives us general indications about the political awareness of these groups, which seems to be gradually increasing.

Respondents were asked in the Gallup surveys about the party meetings they had attended during that election's campaign. Only 15 per cent of whites, 16 per cent of Afro-Caribbeans, and 14 per cent of Asians claimed to have attended and 9 per cent of whites, 11 per cent of Afro-Caribbeans,

Table 42 *Interest and significance of who wins the 1979 general election – by ethnic groups*

	Ethnic group		
	White (10,320) %	Afro-Caribbean (109) %	Asian (111) %
A. *Interest*			
Very interested	44	43	37
Moderately interested	29	25	27
Only a little interested	27	32	36
B. *Significance*			
Matters a lot	53	46	42
Matters a little	18	18	17
Doesn't matter	29	36	41

and just 5 per cent of Asians said they participated in the canvassing. Therefore, all these results show that there is not a significant difference in the various aspects of political participation of different ethnic groups. However, there is one important point to be made here about Afro-Caribbeans and Asians. It appears from the research evidence available that Afro-Caribbeans have a higher degree of 'verbal' interest in politics compared with Asians whose turnout is very high (see p. 61); this no doubt affects the ballot box results. Studlar and Layton-Henry comment on this:

> 'Evidence grows for the depiction of a relatively apolitical but voting Asian population and a somewhat more political but non-voting black population. Especially when political activities involve more chance of direct discussion about politics (i.e. buttons, canvassing), Asians are less willing to become involved than blacks and whites. The Asian electorate is more passive politically than blacks in almost all areas of endeavour except voting.'
>
> (Studlar and Layton-Henry 1984: 22)

However, it is worth emphasizing that between the 1979 and 1983 general elections, the active participation of Asians had increased as had that of the other ethnic minorities because of the interest shown in them by the main political parties. There were also the activities of organizations such as the Anglo-Asian Conservative Society, which by 1983 had 20 local branches and a membership of over 2,000. The number of Asian candidates put forward by the main political parties in 1983 provided another incentive for active political participation by Asians. For example, more than half of the 18 ethnic minority candidates in this election were Asians.

Ethnic sections within political parties

After the 1983 general election, the demand for black sections in the Labour party has grown among some active Afro-Caribbean and Asian members of the party. Some of them claim that ethnic minority support for the Labour party is not being properly acknowledged. As one of them put it, 'With the hard work of some ethnic minority workers of the party the ethnic minority membership of the party has gone up. But there is still racial inequality in the party. That is why we want the black sections to monitor progress.' Many of these activists believe that if there can be sections for women and young people why not for ethnic minorities?

The controversy about the black sections within the Labour party is recent but it has a long history, according to some of the supporters of these sections. However, we would like to deal here with events in this connection just before and after the 1983 general election. In 1981 and 1982 some local ethnic minority groups within the party and the Labour councillors from ethnic minority communities started to organize themselves to get some recognition within the party's hierarchy. For example, they had no representation in the NEC and the House of Commons. With the help of the LPRAG, these activists circulated a model resolution for submission to the Labour party annual conference in September 1983. This move helped to get a debate on a long composite resolution (there were four, originally):

'This conference recognizes that in this unequal society there is no real equality of opportunity and that working class people, women and ethnic minority groups suffer severe discrimination.

Conference notes that our party itself is unfortunately not free from this and therefore accepts the principles of positive discrimination in favour of disadvantaged groups.

Conference instructs the National Executive Committee to set up a working party which:

(a) will produce proposals for necessary constitutional amendments for decision by the 1984 party conference for ensuring greater involvement and more equal representation of disadvantaged groups at all levels of the party;

(b) should give serious consideration for proposals for mandatory inclusion of members of disadvantaged groups on parliamentary shortlists where ever such members apply;

(c) recognizes in particular the right of black members of the party to organize together in the same way as women's sections and young socialist branches;

(d) should include a substantial number of members nominated by affiliated organizations and women's sections.'

(Labour party conference, 1983)

In the same conference an ethnic minority trades union official, James Thakoordin, said

'that the party would lose the votes of coloured people if it continued to exclude them from leading positions. "Your record stinks at times", he said, "You must change your attitudes and bring them in." He pointed out that there were no black faces on the platform and few amongst the trade union delegation. Not enough people have voted Labour at the last election, he said. "They're cheesed off with Labour. The party cannot take their votes for granted." There were too many white councillors in inner-city areas and not enough black parliamentary candidates. "We must get away from being a white and male dominated, chauvinistic and an often racist and sexist Labour party."'

(*Daily Telegraph*, 4 October 1983)

After the conference, discussion about the black sections seemed to be gaining momentum as well as press attention generally, from the ethnic press in particular. But in April 1984 the Labour party leader Neil Kinnock opposed the formation of separate sections of the Labour party for black members. He was speaking to a group of reporters from the ethnic minority press. He said, 'the moment that we move, for whatever benevolent reasons, to some form of segregated membership in the Labour party, that invites a major regression in our efforts to change attitudes in society, and indeed within the Labour movement' (*Guardian*, 11 April 1984).

Despite the open opposition of the Labour leader, his Deputy, Roy Hattersley, and Gerald Kaufman, Home Affairs spokesman, to the formation of black sections within the party, a national conference of supporters of the black sections was convened in Birmingham in June 1984. This was mainly attended by Afro-Caribbeans and was designed to discuss and ratify a draft constitution for a national Labour party black section. In the event it discussed several other issues as well, including the disadvantage and inequality that the ethnic minority population is facing in this country. The argument about the black sections within the Labour party continued until the party conference in October 1984 when the issue was debated. Over 20 constituency labour parties have already informally set up black sections with black representatives on the management committees. These are mainly in London. However, 'black section' activists claim that there are now 35 black sections throughout the country with a total of 1,000 members.

Two ethnic minority candidates, both supporters of the black sections, were nominated for the Labour party's NEC: Diane Abbott, proposed by the Women's Action Committee, and Keith Vaz, put forward by Richmond and Barnes CLP, but neither was elected. However, just before the Labour party conference in 1984 the working party on 'positive discrimination', which was set up as a follow-up to the 1983 conference, published a consultative document which was presented by its chair, Jo Richardson, MP for Barking.

The document, published at the end of September 1984, dealt with broader issues of disadvantage as well as the black sections. It said the party 'should be the political means by which disadvantaged groups, including ethnic minorities, seek emancipation from economic and social constraints. However, our political commitment to racial equality is not borne out by the number and role of black people in the party.' It said that the black sections would make the party more accessible to black people 'who are all too often discouraged from active involvement because of unwelcoming white, male-dominated, jargonistic meetings'. A week later the party conference, which had 18 resolutions calling for the establishment of black sections, debated the issue and the idea was defeated by an overwhelming majority: 5,457,000 votes to 500,000. However, the conference asked the NEC to consult the party and to present firm proposals at the next year's (1985) conference. It was alleged by some ethnic minority activists that there were only eight ethnic minority delegates at the 1984 conference which in itself was a reflection on the party for its lack of representation.

The campaign by some black activists for the formation of black sections within the Labour party continues. It was in this context that in October 1984 a campaign in Hackney was launched to have a black MP and 27 black councillors elected in that area. The organizers of the campaign argued that they wanted to get black people into power and to have a voice in decisions which affect them. The co-ordinator of the campaign, Lester Lewis, said, 'Nearly half of Hackney's population is black, but of the borough's 60 councillors only five are black' (*The Standard*, 4 October 1984). There have been other activities following the Labour party conference decision in 1984 against having black sections. The campaign's leader, Lewisham councillor Russell Profitt, along with other ethnic minority activists, has been persistent on this issue of changing the climate of opinion. The supporters of the black sections must be pleased that the new General Secretary of the Labour party, Larry Whitty has recently voiced his support. He revealed his support in the March, 1985 issue of Labour's journal, *New Socialist*:

'If I were a black member of the party I would be very upset that a party which can accommodate all sorts of special interests in its constitution has nothing for blacks, and I'd have the general impression that the party wants black votes, and to some extent their activity, but no black MPs or parliamentary candidates.'

(Quoted in the *Guardian*, 28 February 1985)

The activists of the National Committee of Labour party black sections have been supporting local activities to give ethnic minorities more say. The Committee supported the efforts of some Asians in Southall to replace the local MP, Sydney Bidwell, in his re-selection by an ethnic minority candidate. The local campaign, in which almost 1,800 new members, mainly Asians, have become members of the Labour party in the last few months, is gaining momentum in this respect. It is led by Madhav Patil, who is Secretary of the Glebe ward in Ealing and the convener of the party's black section. All these activities have resulted in an enquiry into the local Labour constituency party by the National Executive.

The NEC's working party, chaired by Jo Richardson MP, produced its report, *Black People and the Labour Party*, in June 1985. It supported the formation of black sections within the Labour party although some of its members opposed it. But this recommendation was later rejected by the NEC. A compromise proposal was put forward by Eric Heffer MP, seconded by Tony Benn MP, for ethnic minorities to form their own groups which would affiliate to the party like Poale Zion, the Jewish group inside the Labour party. Eric Heffer also suggested that these ethnic minority groups should then be allowed representation on the National Executive, constituency management committees, and other parts of the party structure. This proposal was also rejected by Labour's NEC. It was reported that Neil Kinnock opposed this proposal on the grounds that the party should be able to articulate the views of all people including the ethnic minorities. However, the NEC recommended the setting up of an advisory committee for the ethnic minorities similar to the party's women's and local government committees.

The controversy over black sections continues and it appears that there will be a bitter debate on this issue at the 1985 Labour party conference in October when delegates will have an opportunity to vote on both the recommendations. However, it is expected that the recommendation about the setting up of 'black sections' will be defeated, probably with a smaller margin than in 1984. Some big unions are being persuaded to support the resolution with their block votes, and it is understood that at least one large union, the National Union of Public Employees, with its 600,000 votes, has decided to do so. On the other hand the signs are that the NEC's recommendation about the setting up of an advisory committee will be approved by the conference delegates.

Two further points need to be made here. First, that not all ethnic minorities support the formation of black sections within the Labour party. Second, that some ethnic minority leaders have come out publicly to oppose this move. For example, Rita Austin, a Labour county councillor in South Glamorgan, who was also a Labour party parliamentary candidate in the 1983 general election, has opposed this publicly. She was also member of Jo Richardson's working party and with two other members produced a minority report opposing the setting up of black sections. Rita Austin said: 'Instead a Labour black rights campaign should be set up which would be open to all members' (*South Wales Echo*, 18 June 1985). According to her a recent survey of black communities showed that there was only a small minority support for black sections. A poll of 2,500 Afro-Caribbeans and 2,600 Asians in 50 constituencies with more than 10 per cent black votes showed that 63 per cent were opposed to separate black sections and only 18 per cent were in favour.

There are other ethnic minority activists of the Labour party who oppose the formation of black sections and believe in an 'integrated approach' within the party. As one of them put it, 'if we are seen as a separate group we will always be used as "token" Asians and Afro-Caribbeans when it suits the party. We should support an "integrated approach" otherwise we will suffer in the long run in terms of getting equality of opportunity within the Labour party.'

Four of the most outspoken members of the black sections have recently been adopted as Labour's parliamentary candidates for 'safe' and 'winnable' seats for the next general election. However, the argument about the black sections goes on.

However, so far there has been one casualty of this controversy. Councillor Russell Profitt is at the centre of the clash between the NEC and Lewisham East constituency party. He was selected by the Labour party to contest this marginal Conservative seat at the next general election. But his nomination was declared invalid by the NEC because two members of the black section participated in the selection procedure. It is generally accepted that councillor Profitt is the best choice and he would have been selected even without the inclusion of black section representatives. Now it has become a matter of principle for the supporters of the black sections and for the time being the selection in Lewisham East is deferred, certainly until after the Labour party conference in October 1985.

The Conservative Party is more flexible in accommodating different sections. For example, the Executive of the National Union of Conservative Associations currently has representatives, among others, of women, trades unions, and young people. The party has helped and encouraged the formation of the Anglo-Asian Conservative Society and the Anglo-West Indian Conservative Society and although these do not have a place on the Executive, they have delegate rights to the annual party conferences and are represented at other forums. One could argue that the party accepts the principle of these special interest groups within the wider framework of the party.

The formation of the Anglo-Asian and Anglo-West Indian Societies in the Conservative party is nothing new; the Anglo-Polish Conservative Associations have existed within the party for many years. The receptions and other functions arranged by the Anglo-Asian Conservative Society are well attended by senior politicians of the party. The Prime Minister, Margaret Thatcher, has been to some of them. The society regularly sends delegates to the annual party conference and usually arranges at least one reception during the conference week, in which members of the society meet both party workers from different areas and politicians. Several ministers and other leading figures of the party always attend this reception. The Anglo-West Indian Conservative Society, which is mainly London based, also arranges such functions, but on a smaller scale and infrequently. Some of the receptions of these societies are held at the House of Commons to facilitate MPs' attendance.

In addition to these activities, the Anglo-Asian Conservative Society has a regular newsletter; it lobbies MPs on issues affecting ethnic minorities and others generally and Asians in particular. In brief, the Anglo-Asian and Anglo-West Indian Conservative Societies are treated very much as part of the party and seen as a 'bridge' between the ethnic minorities and the local associations.

Other clubs and associations of ethnic minorities give support to the Conservative party in various ways. The Durbar club, which includes Asian businessmen among its members, recently raised £75,000 for a computer to be installed in the Conservative Central Office. At one of its dinners early this year, its President Narindar Saroop presented a cheque for £10,000 when Margaret Thatcher, at least half a dozen ministers, and several other dignitaries were present. These attendances and the extent of the contributions show that the relationship between the Conservative party and some sections of the Asian community and other ethnic minorities is becoming more permanent and increasingly important. A leaflet distributed at the Conservative party conference in 1984 read, 'The Asian Community is a Conservative Community ... Enable and Encourage them to Play a Fuller Part in Britain's Political and Commercial Life' (Issued by Tory Asians for the Representation Group and Durbar Club).

The Liberal party does not have special arrangements for ethnic minorities within its constitutional framework but its Community Relations Policy Panel has ethnic minority members. It meets regularly to discuss issues relevant to the ethnic minorities and also formulates policies which the party implements to attract ethnic minority members, as well as campaign strategies at elections specially directed at them.

Like the Liberal Party, the SDP has not got any special arrangements for ethnic minorities within the party's constitution. However, it encourages ethnic minority candidates for its National Council. There are currently two directly elected ethnic minority members on the council. The SDP has started a Campaign for Racial Justice which had been asked to nominate two ethnic minorities to the council to make it more broad-based and more reflective of the composition of its membership.

Although in theory the SDP leadership is against separate provisions, in practice it seems to ensure that ethnic minorities are properly represented. David Owen, the leader of the SDP, told a meeting of the Bengali community in Tower Hamlets in April 1984 that ethnic minorities' political participation should be reflected in the number of ethnic minority party office holders and candidates at local and national level. He said,

'Any concept of separate development for ethnic minorities, either in terms of establishing their own political groupings or in having separate status within existing political parties should be firmly rejected as being unacceptable and essentially repugnant to those who want to see a multi-ractial society as a working reality.'

(*Guardian*, 30 April 1984)

It is understandable that many of the ethnic minorities who joined the SDP were initially supporters of the Labour party. But there were others, mainly professionals and intellectuals, who saw some hope for racial equality in this country with the SDP, as its leadership had a good track record on such issues. How things develop for the SDP and its relationship with the ethnic minorities in terms of their membership and other matters will partly depend on its overall potential and performance in the next general election. The same applies to the Liberal party. Many ethnic minority people have approved Alliance policies, but feeling there was no chance that these parties might run the country in the near future have preferred to support one of the two alternatives, the Conservatives or Labour. Although in the 1983 general election, the Alliance gained support among the ethnic minorities it was still not very significant (Anwar 1984a). Furthermore, the formation of any ethnic minority sections within the Alliance parties is certainly not on the cards and there does not seem to be any demand from their ethnic minority members.

The role of ethnic minority organizations

The history of ethnic minority organizations in Britain is as long as the presence of ethnic minorities themselves. For example, there was an Indian Workers' Association in the 1930s (John 1969). Almost 50 years later in 1985 the number of ethnic minority organizations runs into hundreds. They include national, regional, and local organizations based on national and ethnic origins. Some of these organizations are of a welfare, religious, professional, or political nature. Others perform a combination of these roles. Their role in the political context, organizing ethnic minorities and mobilizing support for the political parties, is therefore crucial. These organizations have both 'formal' and 'traditional' leaders (Anwar 1979b: 172–75) and they play their due role in the political participation of ethnic minorities. Young people are, however, sometimes critical of the ineffectiveness of ethnic minority organizations (Anwar 1976). Of course, ethnic minorities are not a homogenous group, and hence their differences are reflected in their organizations.

The activities of the ethnic minority organizations in terms of political participation or as pressure groups take place regularly but their 'overt' role is noticeable at election times. This section concentrates on a selection of examples to illustrate their involvement in this context, as a fuller description would be almost impossible. The same select approach applies to ethnic minority involvement in election campaigns and ethnic press involvement at election times.

We have seen in some detail the role of Pakistani organizations in Rochdale in various elections (Anwar 1979b). For example, in the 1972 parliamentary by-election in Rochdale, apart from meetings with Pakistani leaders, the Pakistanis were addressed by representatives from each of the three parties. Special meetings were held in the local Pakistani cinema. Pakistanis working on night shift in some factories were addressed by the three major party candidates. All three parties displayed and distributed election material translated into Urdu with the help of Asian supporters. Asian interpreters were used throughout the campaign to overcome language difficulties. This pattern of campaign had continued in all successive elections. In 1972 the Pakistani associations, in particular, the Pakistan Welfare Association, held meetings with Pakistanis to make them aware of the danger of the British Campaign to Stop Immigration in general and for Pakistanis in particular. The association asked the Pakistanis to support the Liberal candidate, Cyril Smith, as he was more sympathetic towards their problems. Some Pakistanis were appointed as polling agents and duties on a street-to-street basis were assigned to Pakistani volunteers who made sure that the majority of Pakistanis voted, a technique very much in use in Pakistan, and which resulted in maximum turnout. Later elections in Rochdale have followed more or less the same campaign strategy. Similarly in another local situation in Bradford, Mich Le Lohe has documented ethnic minority participation in election campaigns in various elections (Le Lohe 1975, 1982). All this shows very active participation by the Asian community and a response to the policies of parties both locally and nationally.

However, for a national review in this context, let us begin by looking at the 1979 election which was monitored nationally (Anwar 1980a). In this election, apart from the local efforts of various ethnic minority groups to organize and mobilize support among their members, the different political parties and some national organizations issued political statements in this connection. For example the Standing Conference of Pakistani Organizations (SCOPO) advised its members and other Pakistanis to vote Liberal in constituencies where the Liberal candidate had an advantage, but otherwise to vote Labour. On the other hand, the President of the Confederation of Indian Organizations made a public plea for Asians to vote Conservative (*Daily Telegraph*, 2 May 1979).

The Black People's Manifesto Conference also issued a manifesto on 21 April 1979. It outlined the problems facing ethnic minority communities in Britain and demanded action on 16 specific issues which would promote racial equality. This manifesto was sent to the leaders of the major political parties and to candidates standing in areas with ethnic minority electors (Black People's Manifesto Conference 1979).

At the 1983 general election, many local and national representatives of ethnic minority organizations made statements about their participation. One such organization, the Confederation of Indian Organizations, in conjunction with the West Indian Standing Conference and the Federation of Bangladeshi Organizations, even decided to put forward three ethnic minority candidates as a protest. Tara Mukherjee, one of their spokesmen, said, 'The House of Commons is still not a multi-racial society by any stretch of the imagination. Politicians understand only one language: the cross on the ballot paper. We are not creating a different party or racial group. We are doing it in order to teach a lesson to the political parties not to take us for granted' (*The Sunday Times*, 29 May 1983). Because of some disillusion with the Labour party among ethnic minority activists for not selecting ethnic minority candidates for safe seats, the action of putting forward independent candidates was taken.

The Anglo-Asian Conservative Society played an important role during the 1983 general election campaign. For example, its chair at the time, Narindar Saroop, toured various areas of Asian settlement, including Blackburn, to muster support for the Conservative candidates. Other known ethnic minority leaders were used by other parties to win ethnic minority votes. During the election campaign, it was quite common to see the photographs and messages of ethnic minority leaders in the ethnic press supporting various candidates. In summary, no election campaign in an area of ethnic minority concentration now takes place without the involvement of ethnic minority organizations.

Participation in election campaigns

As the ethnic minority organizations get involved in the political participation so do individual members of ethnic minorities. For example, those who are now party workers or active at election times help to translate election material into various Asian and other languages. Special leaflets are printed in these languages to explain the main points of their party manifesto as well as the candidates' election addresses. Special meetings were arranged by ethnic minority activists for the candidates and visiting party leaders at both the 1979 and the 1983 general elections to meet members of their community. Some of these meetings were arranged at their places of work and places of worship. Generally many workers from ethnic minority communities participated in canvassing a large number of constituencies.[2]

Ethnic minorities had been appointed as polling agents by the political parties in several areas. They also performed various other duties for the parties, as did the white workers. There is no doubt that in the early 1980s ethnic minorities have become part of every election and election campaign and this involvement is likely to grow as more British-educated ethnic minorities come into the field.

Ethnic press involvement

This section should be seen as part of the ethnic minority response, as mentioned in the last two sections, because most of that activity is reflected through the ethnic minority press. The ethnic press had also taken special initiatives to inform their readers about the policies of the major parties. The October 1974 general election was the first occasion when the leaders of the main political parties sent messages to be published in the main Asian newspapers. These messages outlined the policies with regard to ethnic minorities in general, and Asians in particular. In a letter to *Garavi Gujarat*, Harold Wilson, leader of the Labour party, wrote:

'Many of your readers will have welcomed the Labour government's decision, while maintaining necessary control over immigration, that Commonwealth and foreign husbands can join their wives settled in this country, thus ending discrimination between the sexes. They will have welcomed too, the amnesty for those immigrants from the Commonwealth and Pakistan affected by the retrospective provisions of the 1971 Immigrations Act.

They will have appreciated the decision that Uganda-Asian husbands who became separated from their families following the Uganda expulsions would be admitted to Britain to join their wives and children.'

(Garavi Gujarat, 5 October 1974)

Edward Heath, in his letter, began by calling for 'national unity' but moved on to more specific matters:

'Such unity must be irrespective of race or religion, and it is our intention to pursue positive policies which in our view will promote good race relations. This is of course a corporate responsibility. It requires action by government, employers and trade union leaders in their respective fields.

For our part, we shall introduce, in co-operation with the Community Relations Commission and Race Relations Board, a wide variety of projects to advance the welfare of immigrant communities and we shall thoroughly examine the evils of discrimination in employment. More than this though, we will concentrate on the problems of our inner cities so that questions of employment, education, training, housing, transport, race relations and aspects of deprivation can be seen as a total problem to be tackled by a total approach.

On immigration we feel that we must stand firmly on our belief that strict control is necessary. We all condemn the heartless trade in human misery caused by illegal immigration, but equally, abuse of control is unfair, particularly to immigrants who have arrived lawfully. Furthermore, without such control the search for equal opportunities becomes more difficult. Frictions are created at a time when, above all, we need national unity.

However, we have pledged to continue the amnesty commitments (sic) already made, and to uphold the amendment of immigration rules relating to wives and fiancés. We fully recognise that it is just for the rights of wives and husbands to be made equal in this respect, and we will co-operate with the leaders of immigrant communities to ensure that the right of entry of genuine fiancés and husbands of women settled here are (sic) not abused by unscrupulous people.'

(*Garavi Gujarat*, 5 October 1974)

The Liberal party report *Immigration and Race Relations*, published in April 1974, also got coverage in the ethnic press.

Some of the ethnic minority newspapers did not give their support to any party in this election. *Garavi Gujarat* urged voters not to vote for any party, but for candidates who promised to support the cause of immigrants, fiancés, and husbands of Asian girls and representation for Asians in parliament. However, the *Punjab Times* said that the Labour government in the past six months had shown greater understanding of Asians' problems and difficulties, and had made firm decisions about illegal immigrants and husbands of Asian girls in this country. 'We should vote for Labour candidates and in particular for those who take a firm stand against racism and do not just talk.' And *Janomot* gave credit to the Labour government for its decision on illegal entrants and suggested that ethnic minority voters should not lose the opportunity of casting their votes in favour of candidates they support. *West Indian World* also encouraged its readers to vote Labour, although it reported a procession in Brixton in support of the Conservative candidate. In its issue of 4 October 1974 it said, under the heading 'YOU MUST VOTE',

'At the last election in February, West Indian votes helped the Labour party to form the government of the country. One of the main reasons West Indians have voted Labour in previous elections is the fact that they are at the bottom of the economical-social and political ladder of British society. They feel that it is only a real socialist Labour government who intend to carry out their policies rigorously, they will benefit from the sacrifices which will have to be made to put this country back on its feet.

No other minority community is more affected by the social and economic ills of the United Kingdom than the black community. . . .

In the 1970s we are in a position to influence the results of several seats; in a close election our votes can be a decider, as it was in the February poll. We expect to be given the opportunity of an ordinary citizen in the UK. We will back the party we feel will make a genuine effort to solve the problems of the nation as a whole. The party in this election is led by Harold Wilson.'

Many candidates from areas of high concentration also used the Asian press during the election campaign to win the support of Asian voters by listing what they and their parties had done for the Asians in their area and for ethnic minorities in general. The Labour candidates mentioned what the Labour government had done to the benefit of Asian voters for the last six months. These were: reuniting the Ugandan Asian families, the amnesty to those trapped by the retrospective change of the Immigration Act of 1971; and equal rights for non-resident husbands and fiancés of women in this country, to end sex discrimination.

Furthermore, the Labour Home Secretary, Roy Jenkins, the Conservative Shadow Home Secretary, Sir Keith Joseph, and Cyril Smith, representing the Liberal Party, were interviewed on the BBC television Asian programme *Nai Zindagi Naya Jeevan* to explain the policies of their parties to Asian viewers.

Individual candidates made specific attempts to show their interest and sympathy for ethnic minority affairs. The Labour candidate in Southall, Sydney Bidwell, promised in his election address 'An end to witch-hunts of immigrants' and 'Equal rights for British women married to foreign men'. Both Roy Jenkins and Sir Keith Joseph were photographed talking to members of minority groups during the campaign, and they appeared on television and radio programmes with Cyril Smith to discuss the problems facing the Asian community. Several Conservative candidates were reported to have made contact with members of minorities, particularly N. Lyell (Lambeth Central), P. Thomas (Hendon South), T. Stroud (Newham North-East), and G. Finsberg (Hampstead).

R. Patten, the Conservative candidate in Ealing Southall, said in his election address:

'Race Relations in Ealing Southall: Let government be fully aware of the impact made by those of you who have recently arrived here in tens of thousands with different religions, customs and languages. The arrival has caused many problems, both to the newcomers and to the rest of us. These are national problems. So let the national government pay. As your Member of Parliament, I would campaign ceaselessly for financial aid from the government to solve many of the biggest problems here. Meanwhile I will help anyone, sympathetically, with any individual problem.'

In contrast, the Conservative candidate in Ealing North, G. Dickens, said:

'Immigration. In my view we must face facts. Under no circumstances can we continue to allow the present rate of immigration from overseas. It is no longer in the interests of the people of Ealing and their children to subject our schools, housing and other services to the kind of pressures we have experienced for so many years. Depend on me to fight for changes in the immigration laws.'

(Anwar and Kohler 1975)

In the 1979 general election the ethnic press took even greater interest in the election campaign and the participation of ethnic minorities. One Punjabi paper, the *Punjab Times*, advised its readers to exercise discretion and objective judgement in the use of their vote. Its editorial stated that 'The policies and approaches of both the major parties to many problems including immigration are very similar. Given that situation, an individual elector should vote for one which can help him the most at the time of need' (Singh 1979). In *Des Perdes*, one correspondent wrote, 'As active thoughtful citizens, it is our duty despite being Labour voters to stop Labour imposing Tory policies upon us, both locally and nationally' (Singh 1979).

Bengali papers – *Banglar Dak*, *Janomot*, *Jagoran*, and *Bangladesh Weekly* – also covered election issues. The *Janomot* pointed out that of the three political parties, David Steel's Liberals stood out as the only one worth supporting. 'Unfortunately, however, the Liberals stand no chance of forming the next government. The choice before us, therefore, is between two evils, and we have to choose the lesser of the two.' It added that every Bangladeshi should exercise his fundamental right to vote in the general election (*The Asian* 1979).

The Hindi paper, *Amar Deep*, also gave a good coverage of the electoral issues, in particular of those affecting ethnic minorities during the election campaign (*Amar Deep*, April 1979).

Similarly, the Gujarati press gave a good coverage to the election campaign and the general election results. There were full editorials on the election in *Garavi Gujarat* and *Gujarat Samachar*. *Garavi Gujarat* commented that the Tories believe in family life on the one hand but are tightening immigration regulations unfairly on the other. It also provided ample space for readers' discussions of electoral issues before the elections. *Gujarat Samachar* also made considerable efforts to involve its readers in discussions of electoral issues. In the week leading up to the General Election, it brought out a special issue in which it advised its readers to exercise their franchise on May 3 and outlined the policies of the various political parties.

The Urdu press also took a great deal of interest in the 1979 general election and gave extensive coverage to election issues and the campaign. The common message in all six Urdu papers was that Pakistanis should vote in the election. The *Daily Jang* wrote an editorial, 'The May Elections and the Asians', in which, after spelling out the problems facing Asians and their children settled here, it asked its readers to attend election meetings in their areas and ask the respective party candidates for solutions to their problems. The *Daily Jang* also published a survey it had conducted among Asian voters (*The Daily Jang*, 31 March and 2 May 1979). In its editorial on election day, it stressed that the immigration policies of the three political parties would determine the reactions of ethnic minority voters. The *Daily Millat* also published messages and photographs of some candidates; after presenting an analysis of the policies of all political parties, it advised its readers to vote for the Labour Party (*The Daily Millat*, 3 May 1979).

The three Urdu weeklies, *Mashriq*, *Azad*, and *Akhbare-e-Watan* also published editorials about the election and gave extensive coverage to the election campaign generally. The *Mashriq* published manifestos of the three main political parties and in one of its editorials said of the various parties that 'they are all opposed to immigrants and yet they cannot ignore them'. The *Akhbare-e-Watan* also wrote an editorial on 2 May entitled 'The General Election: Britain and Immigrants' in which it reminded ethnic minorities that their votes are important since they have linked their own and their children's future with the destinies of this country. In the *Azad* a correspondent suggested that all Asian voters should demand a statement of intent from candidates in their area to work for the achievement of a just and equitable society (*Azad*, April 1979 issues). The *Ravi* of Bradford advised its readers: 'In the past, Labour governments have not been all that admirable; but compared to the Tories, they have at least done something. Your votes, however, should go to Labour because it is better to have something than nothing at all' (*Ravi*, April 1979). That part of the ethnic press which is published in English also gave extensive coverage to election issues in 1979 especially those concerned with race and immigration (for detailed coverage see in particular, the *Asians*, the *Asian Express*, *India Weekly*, *New Life*, *Race Today*, *West Indian World*, *West Indian Digest*, and the *Post* – all issues published during the campaign).

In the 1983 general election there was so much coverage in the ethnic minority press both in English and Asian language papers that it is impossible to describe it all here. However, it is possible to add new aspects to the above paragraphs about the coverage of the other two elections. For example, this time there was a lot of coverage of the ethnic minority candidates. Several ethnic minority papers featured their profiles. The *West Indian World*, in its issues of 18 and 25 May 1983, covered most of these, as did the *Caribbean Times*. One of its issues in May 1983 advised its readers: 'The vote is yours to do what you like with, but don't forget that used wisely it can bear results which will affect you and your children.' But in the issue just before the election the *Caribbean Times* asked its readers to vote for the Labour party. *The Voice*, another weekly paper, did not urge its readers to vote Labour, but pointed out to them, on 21 May 1983, the importance of the ethnic minority representations: 'The importance of having a black person, regardless of political affinity, to speak for the black community in parliament has been recognised for a long time . . . it will herald a new era of hope and the dawn of political change.' The *Daily Jang* gave extensive coverage as did the other Asian papers.[3] The *New Life* also extensively covered the election campaign, in particular, the participation of ethnic minorities.

The broadcasting media also took an interest, particularly the ethnic minority programmes, in the participation of ethnic minorities in the 1983 general election. For example, among other programmes, the BBC TV *Asian Magazine* programme presented five programmes on the subject before the election on 9 June 1983. It is understood that these were very well received by the Asian community.

In summary, the ethnic minorities participated fully in the campaigns for the 1979 and the 1983 general elections, as well as participating individually in the actual election, through the ethnic minority organizations and through the ethnic minority press. It is clear from the pattern of their participation that in the future their influence in the political life of this country is likely to increase.

8 The anti-ethnic minorities vote

No work about the political participation of ethnic minorities is complete without looking at the electoral performance of those organizations who, among their other objectives, are committed to the compulsory repatriation of all coloured British citizens, including those who were born in this country. The main organization in this category is the National Front, founded in 1966. Like its previous election manifestos, the Front's 1983 general election manifesto entitled *Let Britain Live* stated, 'We will put an end to a multi-racial society in Britain and make it a land fit for our children to grow up in.' It also stated that 'clearly the greatest single contribution which a National Front government will make to law and order will be the repatriation of coloured immigrants and their descendants and dependants' (*The Times Guide to the House of Commons* 1983: 352). The National Front regularly repeats myths, misconceptions, and inaccuracies about immigration and race relations. It has also followed the policy of marches, counter marches, and confrontations, in particular in areas of ethnic minority concentrations.

On the other hand, it is clear that the overt activities of the National Front and the other anti-ethnic minorities organizations have made ethnic minorities more aware of the dangers of these organizations and, as a consequence, more determined to participate in the electoral process to counter the impact of their activities. As one Asian from Birmingham claimed during the 1983 general election, 'I was not a political animal in the 1960s. But, when I saw the literature distributed by the National Front at the October 1974 general election I decided that I must work through the Labour party to counter the anti-immigrant propaganda. I have since convinced several of my friends to do the same. This is important for the future of our children. We must beat them [the National Front] at the ballot box' (the conversation took place in Punjabi and is translated by the author). Such views are held by both ethnic minority and white people.

This chapter reviews briefly the electoral performance of the National Front only since the 1970 general election. The other aspects and activities of the National Front, including its history and to some extent that of the other 'extreme right' anti-ethnic minority organizations, are documented by various other people (Benewick 1972; Hanna 1974; Scott 1975; Husbands 1975, 1983; Nugent and King 1977; Walker 1977; Billing 1978; Fielding 1981; Troyna 1982; and Taylor 1982). It mainly concentrates on the National Front performance in general elections. Where relevant, brief references will be made to some local elections as well.

In the 1970 general election the National Front put up 10 candidates and, on average, they received 3.6 per cent of the votes in the seats they contested. After all the effort and publicity this was a very bad result for the Front. Butler and Pinto-Duschinsky concluded that the National Front activities nationally in the 1970 general election were negligible except in their local press (Butler and Pinto-Duschinsky 1971: 112). However, the situation changed dramatically in the 1974 general elections.

The build-up in 1973 and the results of local elections and parliamentary by-elections did give some indication that the Front might do well at the general election. In constituencies such as Blackburn and Leicester East the 1973 local election results suggested that they might gain as much as 20 per cent of the vote, and in May 1973 at the West Bromwich parliamentary by-election their candidate gained 16.2 per cent of the poll. However, their expectations, based upon local elections or by-elections, were not realized in the general election of February 1974. Their best performances were actually in Leicester and West Bromwich where they had their most encouraging signs but these performances were much worse than one might have predicted.

The National Front's highest number of votes was in Leicester East, where they gained 3,662 votes. With a turnout of 78 per cent, this must be regarded as a reverse considering that in the previous June, when the turnout at local elections was 30 per cent, no less than 4,320 electors within the constituency had voted National Front. The 20 per cent share of the poll, more if one includes votes for the 'Enoch Powell' group, had decreased to 7.4 per cent. It was clearly a disappointment and the candidate went to fight the Loughborough constituency in October 1974.

The West Bromwich seat underwent boundary changes for the 1974 general elections and became West Bromwich East, with a new adjoining constituency of West Bromwich West. In the by-election nine months previously, Martin Webster saved his deposit. In February 1974 the Front candidates in West Bromwich, East and West, slipped back badly and, with their 7.8 per cent and 7 per cent shares, lost two deposits. This general reverse of expectations was also seen in Blackburn where they had had more than 20 per cent of the vote in five wards (Hanna 1974). The 4.2 per cent share in February was one of their best results, but it was much weaker than local election results had suggested.

Looking then at the areas where they had previously been meeting with more success, they suffered a reverse in their fortunes in the general election of February 1974. In fact, they were back where they had been in the general election of 1970, for their average share of the poll was 3.2 per cent in February 1974 as against 3.6 per cent in 1970. This lack of progress in terms of the average share of the vote was perhaps the most balanced assessment of the Front's impact, but one should not ignore the fact that they increased the number of their candidates from 10 in 1970 to 54 in February 1974 and to 90 in October 1974.

Between the two 1974 general elections there were again a few signs that the Front could be making progress. In April 1974, at a local by-election in Bolton, a candidate got 14.6 per cent of the vote and in the parliamentary by-election at Newham South their candidate beat the Conservative candidate with 11.5 per cent of the vote. Compared with February 1974, their actual vote in Newham was down, but their share was up from 6.9 per cent and this was attributed to good organization and the insecurity of the Tate & Lyle workers (*New Statesman*, 31 May 1974).

It is highly likely that the by-election pattern is similar to that of other minority parties who do well between elections and then decline at general elections. Therefore, when it came to the full general election in October 1974, expectations were again not realized. The National Front's candidates in Bolton got 2.4 per cent and 2.7 per cent and their vote in Newham South fell back to 7.8 per cent. The pattern throughout the country was somewhat erratic but, in terms of their share of the vote, the figure was 3.1 per cent (3.2 per cent in February) and they still had not advanced. The total vote had risen from 76,828 in February to 113,344 in October, but this was simply a consequence of having a larger number of candidates. The average vote for the 54 candidates in February 1974 had been 1,422 but the average for the 90 candidates in October 1974 was down to 1,259.

According to one newspaper, Martin Webster regarded this as a decline and blamed the Liberal party for it. The argument was that 'many voters are so non-political that they do not understand the difference between National Front and Liberal policies', and that when Liberals 'intervened' in October, by contesting seats not fought in February, the result was bound to be a decline in the National Front's performance (*Tribune*, 18 October 1974).

Apart from the self-critical implication that many National Front voters were so lacking in conviction and intelligence that their support was politically worthless, the excuse was quite interesting. One can examine it systematically. First, there were 47 seats that the Front fought at both elections, but Liberals 'intervened' in only seven of these. The argument would therefore have to rely upon some dramatic development in only a fraction, about one-seventh, of the constituencies involved.

In fact, there was a dramatic collapse of the Front's vote in these seven constituencies, for in October 1974 the number of votes was around two-thirds of the number in February 1974. But this still cannot be used as evidence against a decline, for the numbers also fell, though slightly and erratically, in the 40 seats that the Liberals contested in both elections. On the other hand, it did seem that the arrival of a Liberal candidate was detrimental to the Front's performance and the suggestion that the Front picks up 'protest' votes which might otherwise go to the Liberals must be taken seriously. Webster himself concedes that he only saved his deposit in West Bromwich because no Liberal was standing (Anwar and Kohler 1975).

Although the Front failed to make an impact at the ballot box in spite of its 144 candidates in the two 1974 general elections, it did receive a lot of publicity. It cost them no less than £21,600 in lost deposits, but the Front gained publicity by qualifying for brief political broadcasts.[1] After the October 1974 election and 90 lost deposits, Martin Webster, the Front's national activities organizer at the time, suggested that it was money well spent for the publicity. 'Where else could you buy five minutes on both television channels for thirteen-and-a-half grand?' (*The Times*, 12 October 1974). After the October 1974 general election and the encouragement, not electoral but in the shape of publicity, which the National Front received, it further increased the number of its candidates at the 1979 general election.

In the 1979 general election, the National Front contested 303 seats and spent £45,300 in lost deposits. Its electoral support on average fell from 3.1 per cent in October 1974 to only 1.4 per cent at the 1979 general election. In parliamentary by-elections, the Front's absolute share of the poll was relatively better, but it also fell from 5.5 per cent in

1968–70 and 6.8 per cent in 1970–73 to 4.4 per cent in 1975–78. The slump in its share of the vote in the 1979 general election reflected a worse performance than in the October 1974 general election when it put up 90 candidates and polled between 2,000 and 3,000 votes in a number of constituencies. Only one candidate, in Newham South, polled more than 2,000 in 1979. The party made strenuous efforts in Greater London by contesting all but four of the 92 seats, as it did in past elections and achieved its highest poll in this area. It obtained its second highest poll in Hackney South and Shoreditch where it polled 1,958 votes compared with 2,544 in October 1974 (it received only 593 votes in 1983).[2]

In assessing the performance of political parties, it is usual to compare the share of the vote achieved in the same constituencies, over two or more elections. Such a comparison assumes constant conditions in these constituencies, that is, no changes in constituency boundaries between elections and no changes in the number of parties involved. There were no boundary changes for the 1979 election but the National Front did not contest 10 out of the 90 seats which they fought in October 1974: this reduced the number of comparable constituencies over the two elections to 80. These, however, had to be further reduced by two because there was a Liberal candidate in these constituencies in 1974 but not in 1979. Therefore, we had a comparable situation in 78 constituencies; in every one of these, the Front's share of votes fell consistently. This fall can be measured by expressing the 1979 share as a percentage of the October 1974 share. Thus, where their share in 1979 was 1.0 per cent but in 1974 it was 2.0 per cent, one could express their share in 1979 as having been 50 per cent of the previous one. This may be called the 'retention rate'.

The average retention rate for the 78 comparable constituencies was 55.6 per cent. In only 12 constituencies did the retention rate exceed 75 per cent and in only eight constituencies did it fall below 35 per cent. There were 11 seats in the industrial North in which the average decline in the National Front's vote was 37.8 per cent of its 1974 share. Indeed, six of the eight seats where this retention rate fell to less than 35 per cent were in the industrial North. In the rest of England, the average retention rates were higher; 53.8 per cent in the South-East, 54.5 per cent in the Midlands, and 59.8 per cent in London. London was the area where the National Front came closest to approaching its 1974 performance and 9 of the 12 constituencies where retention rates exceeded 75 per cent were in the GLC area.

Another method often used to indicate a party's performance, particularly in the popular press, is to refer to their position 'past the winning post'. In the GLC elections in 1977, the National Front was in front of the Liberals in 32 of the 92 London constituencies. In May 1979, the National Front never came anywhere near the Liberals and in 36 constituencies they also fell behind the minority parties. They were beaten by the Nationalist parties not only in the five seats in Wales and the one seat in Scotland that they fought, but also in the three seats where they clashed with Mebyon Kernow in Cornwall. Where they both put up candidates, the Ecology party attracted more votes than the National Front: the Ecology party was ahead of the Front in 17 instances and behind in only seven. There were also 11 other candidates, including two Communists and one Christian 'Stop Abortion' candidate who gained more votes than candidates from the National Front.

Where did the National Front contest in the 1979 general election, and what sort of results did it achieve? When we examine the variations in support of the National Front in different regions a remarkable pattern emerges.

The Front concentrated its efforts in London, contesting 95.7 per cent of seats there, and achieved 2 per cent of the poll. Further, it contested roughly 60 per cent of seats in the South-East and in the Midlands and got less than 1 per cent of the average share of the poll. The Front achieved its lowest level of support in the far north of England (0.72 per cent) and in Scotland and Wales gained 0.23 per cent and 0.57 per cent respectively.

It is interesting to note the constituencies that the Front did not contest in 1979. In the West Midlands, where its share of the vote was relatively good, there were no candidates in Birmingham Ladywood, Handsworth, or Sparkbrook. These three constituencies, according to the 1971 census, had the largest proportion of residents of New Commonwealth origin in the West Midlands area. Ladywood is particularly surprising since in the August 1977 parliamentary by-election the National Front candidate (with 5.7 per cent of the vote) took third place and the Liberal candidate came fourth. It is also interesting to note that the party did not contest either of the two seats in Huddersfield where, 10 years earlier, they believed that they were making a real impact on the population.

There appeared to be an element of inconsistency in the choice of constituencies fought by the Front. First, although in October 1974 they added 36 to the number fought in February 1974, they actually abandoned seven. Second, there were no obvious criteria that could be used to make a logical pattern out of the seats contested. For example, the Front did not concentrate on politically sensitive seats, the marginals, nor did it concentrate on those seats where there were substantial numbers of ethnic minorities. Among the seats they did contest were Bournemouth, Bridlington, Canterbury, Norwich, and South Shields, and among those that they did not contest were Oldham, Preston, Dewsbury, and Warley. Nevertheless, geographically, the areas chosen by the Front displayed not only a strong English bias, but an urban bias which was particularly strong in London. Only one of the 90 constituencies was outside England, and only 13 were not borough constituencies. In the GLC there were 92 seats and the Front fought 37 (40 per cent) of them.

Within the London area the fortunes and the tactics of the Front seemed erratic. They fought Uxbridge in the parliamentary by-election and gained 8.2 per cent of the poll in the last month of 1972, but four months later at the GLC election left it to the Action Party, who gained only 1.7 per cent. In the general election of February 1974, neither party had a candidate, thus giving an impression of inconsistency or incompetence if they and their allies were really trying to build up support for an advance in 1974.

The performance in London in October 1974 indicated both a lack of consistency and a lack of knowledge of their own potential. In February 1974 they fought 22 seats, but in October 1974 they withdrew from two of these and entered another 15. The interesting feature here was that their performance in these new seats was generally better than in those which they fought on both occasions. This may be an example of a 'nine-day wonder', but if it was not then one can only conclude that they were not very good at choosing which constituencies should be fought and not very serious about their electoral gains. It would appear that they fought seats where they had an organization or a candidate willing to stand. These may well not have been the seats with the greatest potential support.

At the 1979 general election the pattern of the constituencies contested and the type of regional support received by the National Front was more or less repeated, although the number of the seats contested rose from 90 in October 1974 to 303 in 1979.

In London the National Front contested 88 of the 92 parliamentary seats. The region showing the highest level of support for the National Front was Greater London. Within London itself, there was also a consistent pattern of support. There were five constituencies in England where the National Front achieved a share of more than 5 per cent of the vote and these were all in the East End of London (comprising the boroughs of Tower Hamlets and adjacent parts of Hackney and Newham).

There were a further 13 London constituencies where their share of the vote exceeded 3 per cent and these were all in the vicinity of that area. This larger area takes in the remainder of Newham and Hackney, the whole of Barking, and part of Islington with Waltham Forest to the north of the river and, to the south of the river, parts of Lambeth, Lewisham, and Southwark.

Within Greater London, the constituencies in which the National Front attracted the smallest share of the poll were also located quite distinctively. If one takes into account the four constituencies that the National Front did not contest and the 16 in which their share of the poll was no higher than 1.2 per cent, a clear pattern emerges. There was an almost unbroken chain of constituencies across the extreme south from Orpington westwards to Twickenham which then follows the river up to Chelsea and north through Kensington and Hampstead to Hendon and Hornsey. In these constituencies they received relatively little support.

The tendency then was for constituencies in the East End to support the Front; the areas in which their share of the poll was low were mainly in the West End, extending to the southern part of London. The 16 constituencies with relatively high National Front support were all won by Labour, and the 16 with relatively low support for the Front, plus the four not contested, were all won by the Conservatives. These geographical and political patterns were themselves associated with social class distribution. This factor was significant in explaining geographical variations in the support the National Front received in London.

Away from London, the association between working-class areas and a relatively large share of the poll for the National Front was not maintained. The cities of Hull and Sheffield, which are predominantly working class and also areas of Labour strength, comprised nine constituencies in which the average National Front share was 0.8 per cent. In Manchester and Liverpool, the National Front contested seven constituencies and their average share of the votes was under 1 per cent. A few examples given in *Table 43* illustrate their declined vote.

On the other hand, at Fylde South, where the Conservatives had the largest majority in Great Britain, the National Front candidate had a better result than his colleagues in the northern cities.

It might be argued that to focus on northern seaside areas and cities with relatively few citizens of NCWP origin could be misleading. The purpose of this analysis, however, is to stress that social class is not by itself an adequate explanation for variations in the level of support for the National Front; other factors such as the presence of ethnic minorities

Table 43 *Percentage of votes cast for the National Front in February 1974, October 1974, and May 1979 general elections by constituency (a select list)*

	February 1974 %	October 1974 %	May 1979 %
Blackburn	4.2	4.4	1.5
Bolton East	2.6	2.4	1.0
Manchester Openshaw	1.8	—	0.6
Preston South	—	1.7	0.6
Liverpool Walton	1.7	—	0.7
Rochdale	3.7	4.1	1.4
Wallasey	—	1.5	0.9
Brent East	—	2.9	1.8
Hackney North and Stoke Newington	3.7	3.7	3.0
Hornsey (Haringey)	—	2.4	0.8
Leicester South	3.0	4.1	1.7

Note: This table includes some of the strongholds of the National Front such as Blackburn, Hackney, and Leicester.

and a reasonably strong group of National Front activists are just as important.

Northern industrial constituencies which have or have had groups of National Front activists and which also have ethnic minorities did not, in any instances, have National Front candidates in 1979 but in 13 such constituencies, the average share of the poll achieved by the Front was only 1.1 per cent. These 13 were all textile towns and returned 11 Labour members, a Liberal and a Conservative, the latter having the smallest majority in the country. This 1.1 per cent share scarcely differs from that in the other cities referred to previously and remained below the average of 1.4 per cent in the four Conservative constituencies in the Blackpool/ Fylde area.[3]

In the East and West Midlands, the level of support for the National Front was higher and its pattern did not differ significantly from that in earlier elections. In the East Midlands, the strongest support, though much reduced, was in and around Leicester. In that city and the two adjacent constituencies where the party put up candidates, the National Front's average share of the vote was 2.5 per cent. In the five comparable constituencies in and around Nottingham, their share was 1 per cent (this was also their average for the rest of the East Midlands).

Within the West Midlands region, the National Front also attracted up to 2.5 per cent of the vote in one area. This area comprised 11 constituencies, nine with National Front candidates, in the five towns of Dudley, Walsall, Warley, West Bromwich, and Wolverhampton. In the rest of that region, including Birmingham and Coventry, the National Front contested 25 constituencies but achieved only 1.2 per cent of the vote.

At the 1983 general election the National Front put forward 60 candidates. All of them lost their deposits. It received only 0.1 per cent of the total votes cast in this election compared with the 0.6 it received at the 1979 General Election with 303 candidates. The Front polled, on average, 1 per cent per candidate compared with its 1.4 per cent at the 1979 General Election. Its highest vote was only 3.7 per cent, at Newham South in 1983.[4]

It appears that the reason that the National Front contested 60 constituencies was once again to get free publicity through the broadcasting time that political parties are entitled to once their candidates number 50 or more. Now, with the deposit increasing from £150 to £500 at the next general election, it remains to be seen if the Front will be able to use this opportunity again.

With the immigration issue out of the political debate, it probably will not be able to field the minimum of 50 or more candidates in the future.

The type of constituencies the National Front contested and the regional pattern at the 1983 general election did not differ greatly from the type of constituencies contested by its candidates at the 1979 general election. But there were far fewer candidates standing for the Front in 1983.

It is worth pointing out that the Ecology Party (with its 107 candidates) and other smaller parties received more votes than the National Front at the 1983 general election. Therefore, the electoral performance of the National Front in 1983 was on the whole disastrous, to say the least.

Before concluding this chapter it will be useful to look at the type of people who stood for the National Front. Mich Le Lohe undertook such an analysis at the 1979 general election, along with some of the analyses used earlier (for details see Anwar 1980a).

It is usually assumed that there were some determined members of the National Front who regularly contested elections, some of these simply for the publicity to be gained. This could be examined by observing the proportion of those who, having fought for the party in the election of October 1974, 'soldiered on' and fought for their party again in 1979. The proportion of this type of candidate was surprisingly low, since only

25 of the 90 candidates who contested the election in October 1974 reappeared as candidates in May 1979. This figure would increase to 28 if we included those who were candidates in either February or October 1974. Those who stand as candidates are normally regarded as being among the top rank of activists; on this criterion, candidates put up by the Front had a 'persistence rate' which was as low as 28 per cent in 1979. This suggests that the party had poor quality 'activists'. Other minority parties had much higher rates of 'persistence'.

The impression that the party had a core of activists derives largely from the fact that it contained 'husband and wife' teams among its candidates. In addition to these married groups, there were candidates who were probably related to each other, standing in adjacent constituencies. Such families are not usually easily identifiable; for instance, six candidates named Jones, five named Smith, and four named Roberts fought the election in 1979. Furthermore, it was known in several other instances, that candidates were related to each other. For example, Mr May and Mrs May who fought two of the Hackney seats and Mr Parker and Mrs Parker, who fought the two Walsall seats were married, and the two Spinks, who fought in Leeds and York respectively, were also married. It would appear from the evidence that 18 families put up more than one of their members as candidates in 1979. On the face of it then, it would appear that the Front contained a number of close-knit activists; in reality, there were so few activists that they had to 'search' within their own families for people who were willing to stand as candidates for their party. In this sense, family participation was also a sign of their weakness.

In addition to the rejection of the National Front at the ballot box, a majority of people wanted it to be banned as a political party because of its anti-ethnic minorities activities and its abhorrent tactics. We asked respondents during our survey whether there were any political parties which they felt should be banned. Over half (57 per cent) felt that there was one party which they would like to see banned. Of these, 88 per cent identified that party as the National Front; 97 per cent of Afro-Caribbeans and 96 per cent of Asians were of this opinion, compared to 79 per cent of our white respondents who also called for it to be banned – an overwhelming response. The only other party mentioned was the Communist Party. Twenty per cent of white respondents, 2 per cent of Afro-Caribbeans, and 1 per cent of Asians would like to see the Communist Party banned (Anwar 1980a).

To conclude then, the widespread view presented by the media that the National Front had been a viable political party like the four main political parties, certainly until the 1983 general election, is not borne out by our evidence, as shown in *Table 44*. It remains a 'one issue party', a 'protest party', and a 'pressure group' against 'coloured' immigration and ethnic minorities settled in this country.

Table 44 *National Front performance at the last three general elections*

General election	No. of candidates	Total votes received	Average votes received %	Percentage of total votes
October 1974	90	113,843	3.1	0.4
1979	303	191,719	1.4	0.6
1983	60	27,062	1.0	0.1

The analysis in *Table 44* clearly demonstrates that, in spite of the publicity which the National Front has received in the media, an over-whelming majority of British people – irrespective of their race and colour – are opposed to its extremist ideology, policies, and tactics. The view that the National Front enjoys a widespread support is a myth. It is totally rejected by the British public at the ballot box, which is the best criterion for estimating the National Front's support.

9 Conclusions and the future

The concentration of ethnic minorities in several areas of Britain has maximized their importance as electors. They are becoming increasingly involved in British politics. Their numbers, turnout patterns, and voting behaviour in areas where they are concentrated are having an increasingly significant impact on the outcome of any election in those areas.

However, the participation of ethnic minorities in the political process must be seen in the wider context of our society, in which racial disadvantage and racial discrimination persist. As the then Home Secretary, Leon Brittan, said in 1983:

> 'The causes of the difficulties that exist between members of different races in Britain are complex. But the fact is that racial discrimination and racial disadvantage are a daily reality for far too many black and brown people in this country. This is disgraceful, not least because it is by no means what is desired by the majority of the population of these islands. But the reality remains. It is a hard fact that ethnic minorities suffer disproportionately from unemployment; there is incontrovertible research evidence to back up individual experiences of discrimination in recruitment or selection.'
>
> (Speech made in Bradford on 22 July 1983)

Similarly, political parties as part of our society are not free of prejudice and discrimination on the part of their members against the ethnic minorities. These could be conscious or unconscious acts. Some ethnic minority members have publicly complained about such treatment. For example, a Labour councillor, James Hunte (a West Indian), from Birmingham was suspended by the Perry Barr Labour party for 12 months when he made statements to newspapers 'accusing the Perry Barr Labour party of blatant racism (*Caribbean Times*, 3 February 1984). In its comment column the *Caribbean Times* wrote:

> 'The Labour party has collected black votes unchallenged for the last 30 years. Today the black community has decided to cash in its chips, we need to see the colour of the Labour party's intentions. What is happening in the Perry Barr Constituency Labour party is no accident, the day of reckoning has come. Lord Pitt endured the largest swing against Labour in a safe seat. It was not an accident, it was simply that there were many racists among Labour voters.'
>
> (*Caribbean Times*, 3 February 1983)[1]

Another Labour councillor, Bishan Das from Wolverhampton, has complained that because of his colour he was not made the mayor on three occasions after repeated promises by the ruling Labour group on the council that he would be. He said that as a protest, he would not stand in the next local council elections (*Daily Jang*, 21 February 1985). However, councillor Das was later asked by the Labour group leader in Wolverhampton to reconsider his decision.

The debate about the black sections within the Labour party is also partly based on the assumption that there is discrimination at different levels of the party which hinders the progress of ethnic minority members within its hierarchy. Thus, at the Labour party conference in 1984, some speakers during the debate on the 'black sections' issue made allegations of such racial discrimination in the party (*The Morning Star*, 26 September 1984).

The Conservative party has also been accused of 'extreme right' infiltration. A report prepared by the Young Conservatives revealed that National Front members had joined the party. A BBC Panorama programme which used this report discussed the whole issue of the 'extreme right's' activities within the Conservative party. These allegations were denied by the party hierarchy and its chairman attacked the Panorama programme by calling it 'outrageous'. A complaint was also lodged about the programme. Some other incidents of racial prejudice had been mentioned by some of the ethnic minority candidates who stood in the 1983 general election for the Conservative party. However, generally it appears that those ethnic minorities who have joined the Conservative party tend to be less critical of the party than some ethnic minority activists in the Labour party.

The political parties need to educate their own members and try to stamp out any racial prejudice and racial discrimination which exist within the parties. They also ought to set an example for others of promoting racial equality and good relations. It is by doing this that ethnic minorities would be encouraged to join the political parties and become integrated into the political process without any fear of harassment, or less favourable treatment. As highlighted in previous chapters, the importance of ethnic minorities in the political process is unquestionable. However, the integration of ethnic minorities into the political process requires their 'effective' representation and involvement and not 'tokenism' as has happened so far. They need to feel equal and to participate fully in the decision-making process. This will in turn, make them feel that they are accepted as full citizens of this country, rather than a 'problem' and one which is to be 'deplored'. The question arises, how could this be achieved?

The process obviously has to be a two-way effort: the political parties to open their doors to the ethnic minorities and welcome them as members by removing all the obstacles; and the ethnic minorities to feel free to join the political parties and take initiatives without any fear of rejection or prejudice. The political parties need to make sure that their ethnic minority members also get an equal chance to represent the party at all levels to make their representation effective. We can learn from the United States, where concerted efforts in the 1970s both by the political parties and the blacks helped to achieve a breakthrough in the political process for blacks. As a result, the representation of blacks increased dramatically. A report of the Joint Centre for Political Studies in Washington published just before the 1984 American presidential election looks at various aspects of this process (Cavanagh 1984).

There were 17.8 million blacks of voting age in the United States in November 1982. This number constituted 10.5 per cent of the total voting-age population of the United States. The States of New York, Texas, Illinois, and California had an estimated black electorate of 1 million or more (New York 1.6 million). A little over half (52.9 per cent) of America's black voting-age population lives in the South. But what sort of representation have blacks achieved in the political life of the United States?

There is no doubt that in the last 13 years the number of blacks elected for various offices has increased. For example, the overall number of black elected representatives increased from 1,469 in 1970 to 5,606 in 1983. The important breakthrough came in the number of black congressmen and state representatives and city council members. Between 1970 and 1983 the number of black members of congress doubled from

10 to 21 and the number of state representatives increased from 137 to 290 in the same period. But the dramatic change took place in the city council members where the number of blacks shot up from 552 in 1970 to 2,030 in 1983. The number of black state senators increased from 31 to 85 between 1970 and 1983 and the number of black mayors from 48 to 247 in the same 13 years. This illustrates a steady but important progress by blacks in the political life of the United States.

Progress has been made by increasing the registration of blacks as electors and by the efforts of the political parties to make black representation effective. It was estimated that grass-roots mobilization efforts added 600,000 blacks to the electoral register between 1980 and 1982. As a consequence of their large numbers, for the past few years blacks have actually influenced the outcome of elections in some areas.

Like the Labour party support among ethnic minorities in Britain, the Democratic party in the United States has been receiving the majority of the black vote. But blacks have not always been strong supporters of the Democratic party. Before the 'new deal' era, blacks were just as solidly identified with the Republican party, 'the party of Lincoln', which had abolished slavery during the Civil War. Even today, there are many blacks supporting Republican candidates. Some people believe that in the United States,

'the status of the black vote as a consistent bulwark of the Democratic coalition presents an opportunity to the Republicans. Without black votes in several large States, the Democrats could not hope to attain a majority in the Senate or in Presidential elections. Similarly, the presence of safe Democratic seats in largely inner-city districts affords the Democrats a cushion in assembling a majority in the House of Representatives. Substantial Republican inroads into the black vote would all but eliminate the majority status of the Democratic Party. Thus, the Democrats cannot afford to take the black vote for granted.'
(Cavanagh 1984: 5)

It could be argued that in Britain, with an even distribution of ethnic minority votes between the two major political parties, the Conservatives could win more inner-city parliamentary seats. Like the Democrats in the United States, the Labour party in Britain cannot afford to take the ethnic minority vote for granted. In fact, as Chapter 5 demonstrates, wherever efforts have been made by other parties' candidates and officials, ethnic minorities have voted for them, for example in Rochdale, Croydon North-East, Watford, Bradford West (in the 1970s), etc. In addition to the policies of parties and the links of their candidates with ethnic minorities in their respective areas, questions are being raised by many ethnic minorities. 'What do we get as a result of our electoral support?'; 'Are we becoming part of the decision-making process?'; 'How do political decisions affect ethnic minorities?' Because political decisions lead to political loyalties, the policies and attitudes of a particular party generally, as well as towards ethnic minorities in particular, are important. For example, some Ugandan Asians are strong supporters of the Conservative party because the Conservative government admitted them to Britain when they were expelled from Uganda by President Amin in 1972. By contrast the Labour government in 1968 rushed through parliament the Commonwealth Immigrants Act to stop the entry of Kenyan Asians with British passports which was resented by ethnic minorities.

In the light of the American experience, we need to find out how this could be achieved in Britain so that parliament and local elected councils reflect the multi-racial nature of our society in the 1980s. As the Home Affairs Committee of the House of Commons noted in its report, *Racial Disadvantage*, 'It is by successful participation in the political system rather than through separation or special representation that the political future of Britain's ethnic minorities must lie' (House of Commons 1981, Paragraph 76). In this context, as mentioned in Chapter 3, both electors and political party candidates we interviewed rejected the idea of separate parties for ethnic minorities (Anwar 1980a). They clearly would like ethnic minorities to participate in the existing political parties, as is already happening to some extent. However, to make the representation of ethnic minorities in Britain 'effective' some steps need to be taken. The following points are relevant in this connection.

1 Ethnic minorities should join the political parties and they should be encouraged to do so.
2 After joining the political parties, ethnic minority members should seek office.
3 Ethnic minorities need to become party candidates and get elected.
4 Ethnic minority candidates should be selected for 'safe' and 'winnable' seats as well in the 'normal' way.
5 Ethnic minority candidates should not be selected from only the ethnic minority concentration areas.
6 Ethnic minority candidates should not be seen as representatives of only their own communities but of all residents where they live, contest, and win.

7 The political parties should not just project their ethnic minority candidates as 'ethnic minorities' but as 'candidates of the party' with certain special qualities and qualifications like other candidates, for example, economists, lawyers, scientists, etc.

8 Once elected, ethnic minority MPs and councillors should represent the interests of all their electorate, not just the interests of ethnic minorities.

9 Political parties need to monitor progress of the ethnic minorities' involvement in the parties.

Let us look at some of these points in detail by using the Jews in Britain, not more than half a million in numbers, as an example of success in the political process. There are at present about 30 MPs of Jewish origin. There are several Jews in the House of Lords; four Jews are members of the Cabinet; and some have become Members of the European Parliament (MEPs). It is a great achievement for a small community and a good example of political integration.

It must be remembered that Jews in Britain started their political participation first fighting for the Jewish emancipation and admission of Jews to parliament. It was not easy. Jews were granted the franchise in 1835. The first Jewish MP, David Solomons, took his seat in 1851. He became the first professing Jew to sit in parliament; Lionel Rothschild was elected in 1847 but he refused to take oath. After the issue of oath was resolved, four professing Jewish MPs, all Liberal, were elected in 1859–60. Geoffrey Alderman has described the struggle of Jews to get into the British parliament (Alderman 1983). He points out that the message from the community leadership was always for Jews to join the political parties, but not necessarily a particular one. The same applied to casting their votes. As the *Jewish Chronicle* wrote in 1951 in a leading article, British Jews would 'cast their votes as individuals and will support the party of their choice, not on the basis of communal interest, but in accordance with their view of the great issues and policies affecting Britain's well being' (*Jewish Chronicle*, 13 January 1951, quoted in Alderman 1983: 151). This policy of neutrality continues even today.[2]

Although most Jews joined the Liberal and then the Labour party initially, slowly the majority have now moved to the Conservative party and other political parties. It was the first time in British political history that at the 1983 general election more professing Jewish MPs were elected for the Conservative party (17) than the Labour party (11). The highest number of Jewish MPs (46) was elected in 1974. The majority of them belonged to the Labour party (35 Labour, 10 Conservative).[3]

The same applied to the Jews' voting patterns. In the recent past the Jews voted overwhelmingly for the Labour party, but now their votes are divided between the main political parties.

As far as Asians in Britain are concerned, their occupational trends and other values, such as ownership and emphasis on family life, are believed to be more relevant to the Conservative party philosophy. They are, therefore, seen as 'natural' Conservatives. As one leaflet mentioned, 'By nature and tradition, the Asian community reflects Conservative values' (TGRG leaflet distributed at the Conservative party conference, 1984). Margaret Thatcher also remarked on this:

> 'The Asian communities living here believe in home ownership. They believe in the value of hard work. They believe in savings. They recognize the importance of family life and of good schooling for their children. They have a strong belief in spiritual as well as material values. These are all the things Conservatives believe in.'
>
> (Conservative Central Office publication)

Due to these factors and the efforts of the Conservative Central Office, as with the Jewish community the original tendency toward Labour is being eroded as Asians perceive increasing affinity with the Conservative party.[4] But it must be mentioned that they are also joining and supporting the Liberal and SDP parties. This pattern of support applies to some extent to other ethnic minority communities as well.

Ethnic minority candidates, should not only be seen as representative of their own communities but also as 'party candidates'; they should be projected by the political parties not as ethnic minority candidates but as candidates for the political parties, representing all residents, when they stand in elections. Political parties need to make sure that their white majority electors get used to the ethnic minority candidates representing the parties, not standing as 'token' ethnic minority candidates. Here again, if we look at the Jewish experience, except where the target group was Jewish electors the ethnic identity of Jewish candidates was rarely mentioned in the campaign literature, or in any other way. Admittedly, the ethnic origin of Asian, Afro-Caribbean, and other ethnic minority candidates is difficult to hide because of their colour. However, they need not be projected as such by the political parties, as has happened with several ethnic minority candidates in the past. Most of the publicity that Pramela Le Hunte received in the press as a Conservative candidate for

Ladywood at the 1983 general election emphasized that she was an Asian standing for the Conservative party, rather than simply a Conservative candidate.

In Chapter 6 the performance of ethnic minority candidates has been presented. Two points are worth making here: first, that Independent and fringe party ethnic minority candidates perform very badly in terms of receiving voters' support and, second, that, except in the case of Dr Pitt in 1970, no ethnic minority candidate had been given a 'safe' or 'winnable' seat. Some have argued that Paul Boateng at the 1983 general election got a 'winnable' seat when he contested Hertfordshire West for the Labour party (FitzGerald 1983). However, because of the dispute at the time of his selection and the adverse publicity he consequently received with the divided Labour supporters, he had little chance of winning that seat. He came third behind the Alliance candidate and the seat was won by the Conservatives.

Nevertheless, the overall performance of ethnic minority candidates at the 1983 general election demonstrates that they are being accepted by the white electors as 'party' candidates. Furthermore, ethnic minority voters now do not vote on ethnic lines but on a party basis (Anwar 1984a). But, at the end of the day, no candidate, whether ethnic minority or white, could win an 'unwinnable' seat. If political parties are serious about the equality of opportunity and feel that ethnic minorities should become part of the parliamentary decision-making process, they must take appropriate steps in this connection. Unless corrective action is taken, as has happened for blacks in the United States at all levels of representation in the last 20 years, the British parliament might well remain all-white. If no ethnic minority candidate is elected in the next general election, there will be a gap of almost a century since the election of the first ethnic minority MP, for the Liberal party in 1892.

Some political party leaders have made statements in the recent past that in the next general election some MPs will be elected from the ethnic minorities. For example, Mr Neil Kinnock, Leader of the Labour party, said in a speech (which was delivered on his behalf by Max Madden, Labour MP for Bradford West), 'I have no doubt that when we form the next government in Britain, there will be Labour Members of Parliament from the ethnic minority communities who will play their full part in building a prosperous, peaceful and just society' (speech for the 9th Annual Lecture organized by a Bengali weekly, *Jagoran* and *Asian Herald* (English) in London on 12 March 1985). On another occasion Neil Kinnock had said that it was a 'matter of mathematical fact that in the next parliament we will have as many as six or seven black MPs' (*Guardian*, 11 April 1984).

Bearing in mind the importance of the ethnic minority vote for the Labour party and the pressures from the 'black sections' lobby, such statements from the leadership seem appropriate. So far four ethnic minority parliamentary candidates have been selected for 'safe' or 'winnable' seats for the Labour party for the next general election. But the other three main parties have not yet followed suit.

However, as mentioned in Chapter 6 most of the ethnic minority candidates in the 1983 general election who stood for the main political parties generally performed like any other candidate for their respective parties. This pattern was confirmed by the exit poll data which compared the relative share of the vote gained by each candidate against white and ethnic minority voters. The results show that if ethnic minority candidates are given 'safe' or 'winnable' seats they will win like any other candidate.

When some ethnic minority MPs are elected their performance as MPs representing the interests of all their constituents and their party will undoubtedly be very important. As the first few MPs from the ethnic minorities they will be watched closely both by the 'majority' electorate and by their respective parties. Their success will open doors for other ethnic minority MPs. But their failure or mistakes will delay the entry of more ethnic minorities to the House of Commons. Dr Pitt's defeat in the 1970 general election, when he lost a 'safe' Labour seat, is a good example in this context which has up till now frightened the main political parties from giving an ethnic minority candidate a 'safe' seat from fear of losing it. However, political parties need not worry any longer, as ethnic minority candidates are now being accepted by both white and ethnic minority voters.

The last point to be made concerning ethnic minority candidates is about the type of constituencies where they are selected. Political parties generally tend to select them in the ethnic minority concentration areas. This is a wrong policy in the long run for several reasons. First, ethnic minorities are not a homogenous group; they now tend to vote on a party basis and their votes would therefore be divided; second, this policy is seen by several ethnic minority political activists and others as 'tokenism' and 'patronizing'. Also the ethnic minority candidates as 'party' candidates should be exposed to 'snow white' areas and in this way white electors will get used to them. This policy will also help to demonstrate that the political parties are serious about their ethnic minority candidates and that they are not just putting them forward to get ethnic minority votes.

Such moves will also be good for community relations in general where ethnic minority MPs represent their predominantly or exclusively white constituents. That is the breakthrough that is needed to provide equality of opportunity in the electoral politics at the parliamentary level. The time is right for such a move. This does not mean that ethnic minority candidates should not be selected in the ethnic minority concentration areas in the normal way. This also must happen.

Although some slow progress has been made in terms of ethnic minority representation at local council level, as presented in Chapter 6, it is still, in the main, in the ethnic minority concentration areas. A breakthrough on the lines suggested in the previous paragraph is needed at local council levels as well, and further progress must be made to increase the representation of ethnic minorities in the areas of their settlement.

One other relevant point to be mentioned here is the question of proportional representation and, if it was introduced in Britain, how ethnic minorities would benefit in terms of their representation in parliament. The system of proportional representation would not benefit ethnic minorities as a separate group all that much. However, if it were introduced in Britain in the future, they would benefit through the existing political parties. Since there is no chance of ethnic minorities organizing themselves as a political party and it would not be in their interests to do so, proportional representation would not be directly favourable to the ethnic minority representation. But those, for example, with the Alliance parties would benefit.

However, it is ironic that, with the present system, in the 1983 general election the Alliance with its 25.4 per cent share of the total votes won only 23 seats, while the Labour party with 27.6 per cent won 209 seats and the Conservatives with 42.4 per cent of the total votes returned 397 MPs. Under the present system, despite the Conservative party's great majority of seats in the House of Commons in the 1983 general election it had received only 42.4 per cent of the national votes cast (which was only 30.8 per cent of the electorate). With the proportional representation system, if seats had been divided according to the votes received by different parties in 1983, the Conservatives would have won 285 (−111), Labour 180 (−29), and the Alliance 160 (+137) seats.

Under the present system, at the 1983 general election on average a Conservative MP was elected by 32,777 votes, a Labour MP by 40,464 votes, but an Alliance MP by 338,286 votes. The supporters of the proportional representation system are raising the question, 'Is this fair?'

A system of proportional representation based on multi-member constituencies with preferential voting by single transferable vote (STV) would be welcomed by many ethnic minorities, because by this system the state of seats won by parties in parliament would help to reflect their support among the voters. In this way no single party would be able to secure a parliamentary majority without getting 50 per cent of the popular vote.

Under the present system many ethnic minorities do not find the Liberal and the SDP parties attractive in terms of political gains because they know that the Alliance parties stand no chance of forming a government in the near future. Under this electoral system, the Alliance parties certainly are losers. However, many ethnic minorities who are sympathetic to these parties, and some who have joined them and voted for them, believe that, if proportional representation were introduced, the situation would be different. What could also benefit ethnic minorities through the existing political parties and the electoral system is multi-member constituencies, like some local wards, where political parties will perhaps be more willing to put forward some ethnic minority candidates as part of their 'slates'. This system has worked at local election level and would no doubt work at parliamentary level as well.

Like the United States, where increased registration among blacks helped gradually to increase their representation in the decision-making process, the increased registration of ethnic minorities in Britain in the last few years and in the future is likely to do the same. The tendency among British ethnic minorities, in particular Asians, to higher turnout, makes them important voters. The Asian turnout is sometimes double that of their white neighbours, as outlined in Chapter 4. If the present pattern of voting among ethnic minorities continues, and with the efforts of the Conservative party, many Asians, for example, will join the Conservative party and many more will be voting for its candidates; like the British Jews, some of them will eventually become Conservatives. The growing dissatisfaction with and alienation from the Labour party among many ethnic minority activists in the recent past means that the chances of ethnic minorities joining the Conservative party and the Alliance parties in increasing numbers cannot be ruled out.

There is also the added factor in favour of the Conservative party that it is the party in power and is therefore in a position to formulate and implement policies of relevance to the interests of the ethnic minorities. Such policies could attract loyalty to the Conservative party from the ethnic minorities. In conjunction with the Conservative philosophy about the family, ownership, and small businesses, etc. and the growing number of ethnic minority professionals, the Conservative party stands a good chance of winning support from many Asians and other ethnic minorities. However, in the near future the majority of ethnic minorities are likely to vote for the Labour party.

Now that the immigration issue is no more a 'political issue' in terms of numbers, with no primary immigration taking place from the New Commonwealth countries and Pakistan, it is hoped that in future immigration as a political issue will not be debated at the Conservative party conferences. Certainly it has no chance of becoming an election issue. Even in the 1983 general election, immigration 'dropped off the bottom of the political agenda' (Crewe 1983). Now, with the publication of the CRE report *Immigration Control Procedures* (1985) and the formation of the new All-Party Parliamentary Group on Race Relations,[5] discussion should shift from the numbers to the question of equality for those dependants who have a right to enter this country under the already very strict immigration controls.

On the other hand, some of the previous policies of the Labour party concerning ethnic minorities, such as the 1968 Commonwealth Immigrants Act, are still being criticized by many ethnic minorities and supporters of the Labour party. The promised repeal of the Immigration Act 1971 by the Labour party was not even proposed by the 1974–79 Labour government.[6] As one Asian Labour party activist said:

'How can you trust the future Labour government to repeal the Immigration Act 1981 and the Nationality Act 1981 when their previous record shows that they make such noises only when in opposition but, when in power, they are frightened to take any action because of their racist supporters. I am watching the Conservative government closely for its policies about race relations and in the light of its performance I, along with my many friends, might soon join them (Conservative party). At least they do what they say they will do. The decision about the Ugandan Asians by the Heath government is a good example. With them (Conservatives) you know where you stand. If the Labour party is not careful, in the next general election more Asians will be voting Conservative than Labour!'

This feeling is shared by some other ethnic minority supporters of the Labour party as well as by many whites who take an interest in ethnic minorities.

As far as the importance of the ethnic minority vote is concerned, it has publicly been recognized by the leadership of the main political parties as referred to in Chapter 6. With the 'immigration' issue out of the political debate, in future the attention of the political parties would and should move to the question of equality of opportunity in the political process and other institutions in society. This must be monitored both within the political parties and outside institutions. As has been confirmed by recent surveys, white people think that ethnic minorities should be treated the same (Anwar 1981b). Most white people now accept Britain as a multi-racial and multi-cultural society and there is no chance of anti-immigrant organizations such as the National Front succeeding. As we have seen in Chapter 8, British voters have already rejected the National Front and similar 'extreme' parties at the ballot box. At the 1983 general election the National Front with its 60 candidates received only 0.1 per cent of the total votes cast. This was 0.5 per cent lower than its 1979 general election result. It is encouraging that white people now see ethnic minorities as an integral part of society: almost half of them are now British-born, many others have grown up here, and the rest are almost all British citizens.

On the other hand, to increase ethnic minority representation in the political process, and looking at the Jewish experience in this connection, the ethnic minorities need to join the political parties in greater numbers, seek office, and work hard through the political parties' hierarchy to become candidates and get elected. They also need to get involved actively in trades unions, as many MPs for the Labour party are sponsored by the unions. It is not good enough to become active and get involved at election times only. The process of political party membership among ethnic minorities has actively started in several areas, for example, Bradford, Leicester, and Southall. Political parties must become accessible to ethnic minorities; since in certain areas they are numerous, their vote does count. Without ethnic minority participation in the political process, the chance of equality of opportunity and good race relations is diminished.

Finally, we must rise to the challenge of becoming a truly multi-racial and multi-cultural society. Other countries are watching us. The House of Commons is still all white. We hope that at the next general election it will more closely reflect the multi-racial make-up of our society.

Notes

Chapter 1

1 The 1981 census showed that nearly 3.4 million people were born overseas. The majority (1.89 million) of these were whites. Over 607,000 were born in Ireland, 153,000 in the Old Commonwealth (Canada, New Zealand, and Australia), and about 1.3 million in other countries in Western Europe. Almost 100,000 white people were born in the Indian sub-continent and African countries while their parents were on overseas service. The remaining 1.41 million were 'coloured' (ethnic minorities), having been born in the New Commonwealth countries and Pakistan.

Also see Home Office, *Control of Immigration: Statistics United Kingdom, 1984* (1985) for details about immigration.

2 A Home Office report, *Racial Attacks* (1981), showed that the incidence of inter-racial victimization was much higher for the ethnic minority population, particularly Asians, than for white people. Indeed, the rate for Asians was 50 times that for white people and the rate for Afro-Caribbeans was over 36 times that for white people.

3 The 1981 census did not provide us with the complete picture of the ethnic minority population in Britain because an 'ethnic' question was not asked in the census. Because the information collected was based on birthplace and was asked without a question on parents' birthplace, those UK-born ethnic minorties who have formed separate households from their overseas-born parents were not identified in the 1981 census. This means that, for areas like Cardiff, Bristol, and Liverpool, the 1981 census information about ethnic minority groups is meaningless. The same will be true for other areas if the 1991 census does not include an ethnic question.

Therefore, any information used in this book from the 1981 census regarding ethnic minorities should be treated as an under-estimate. Furthermore, we are already in 1985 and thus the size of the ethnic minority population has gone up since the 1981 census.

Chapter 2

1 The media had used the riots to sensationalize the immigration issue. A Gallup
   Poll at the time showed that 92 per cent of those questioned had read about the
   riots (September 1958). Another national poll carried out after the riots for the
   Daily Express found that almost 80 per cent of those interviewed wanted
   immigration control and only 14 per cent did not want to see any action taken.
   However, the debate about the immigration control continued into the 1964
   general election and it was made an election issue by some candidates.

   Although immigration was not an issue in the 1959 general election, Sir
   Oswald Mosley as a Union Movement candidate in the North Kensington
   constituency (which included Notting Hill) tried to exploit the previous year's
   riots. He did not succeed. He was bottom of the poll and lost his deposit.
2 The detailed comparative figures for electoral registration for Asians, Afro-
   Caribbeans, and whites are presented in Chapter 4. It is estimated that almost
   one-fifth of the Asians in some areas were not on the register.
3 In the last few years leaders of the other three main political parties have made
   similar statements. Some of these are presented in Chapter 6.

Chapter 3

1 The main objective of these surveys was to look at the attitudes of ethnic
   minorities and white respondents to race relations generally. There were also
   questions about different aspects of respondents' lives: discrimination, the
   police and community relations, and race and community relations organizations.
2 This shows the political integration of ethnic minorities in terms of recognizing
   the main and important political issues at the time of the survey. Furthermore,
   'race relations' as an issue has never seriously become part of the British
   political agenda. However, the issue of 'immigration' has consistently received
   the most attention from politicians and the media. Two surveys at the time of
   the 1983 general election (BBC-Gallup election survey 1983 and the Harris
   survey 1983) also revealed that ethnic minorities ranked unemployment as the
   most important issue (No. 1).
3 American political scientists make a distinction between 'position' issues and
   'valence' issues. In simple terms, a position issue is one on which parties and
   voters take up positions for or against and it is normally an ideological issue.
   Valence issues are those on which parties and voters agree. The outcome
   usually depends on which party is more likely to maximize whatever it is that
   everyone is agreed on.

Chapter 4

1 It is estimated, based on the 1981 census figures, that in 1985 there are almost
   1.8 million eligible ethnic minority voters in the United Kingdom.

2 At the time of writing the second such meeting was being planned for London.
3 The indications are that the reasons for non-registration are complex, and unless we have detailed interviews with those who do not register, we will not be in a position to suggest effective remedial action.
4 The national turnout for all voters was 72.7 per cent at the June 1983 general election. This means that the Asian turnout was even higher than the national average. Furthermore, the close analysis of results shows that in some constituencies the Asian turnout was over 90 per cent. These included Bristol East (92 per cent), Ealing Acton (93 per cent) and Southampton Itchen (94 per cent). Comparative figures for non-Asians in these areas are presented in *Table 20*. These differential rates of turnout clearly demonstrate the electoral significance of Asian voters.

Chapter 5

1 Constituencies where the number of ethnic minority electors was approximately larger than the majority in the February 1974 general election. The same definition applies to the subsequent elections in this book.
2 At the 1983 general election the pattern of support among Asians for the Conservative party candidates in some of these constituencies was similar to the 1979 results presented in *Table 32*.
3 The Liberal party received 5 per cent of the ethnic minority vote at the 1979 general election; however, the Liberal/SDP Alliance attracted 11 per cent of the ethnic minority vote at the 1983 general election in areas covered in our surveys. It appears that the additional ethnic minority vote for the Alliance in 1983 came from the Labour party supporters and not from the Conservative party – following the general pattern of voting in that election.
4 Hamid Qurashi was the only SDP councillor in Bradford who was elected in this election. In the beginning of 1985 he resigned his seat because of personal reasons and it was once again won by the Labour candidate, Mr Riaz, in February 1985.
5 I gather from my contacts in the political parties that the number of ethnic minority candidates is likely to increase substantially from 1985 to 1987 for local elections.

Chapter 6

1 The Union of Muslim Organizations in the UK and other ethnic minority organizations sometimes also arrange fringe meetings or receptions at party conferences which are normally attended by important politicians and trade unionists. The interest taken in the activities of these groups by the party leadership shows their importance in the electoral process.
2 Zerbanoo Gifford, a councillor from Harrow, is the new chair for the panel.
3 In a BBC TV interview (with Terry Wogan) Rochdale MP Cyril Smith claimed that he usually attracts almost 10,000 as his 'personal vote', which is

almost half of the 21,858 votes he received at the 1983 general election. My research in Rochdale over the last 13 years shows that the majority of Asian votes Cyril Smith receives are 'personal votes'. This pattern of voting among Asians applies to some other candidates as well where they have created good contacts with the Asian community, irrespective of their general party support among Asians.

4 The pattern of District Council elections varies from year to year. The Metropolitan District Councils hold elections normally for one-third of the seats every year except when boundaries are re-drawn or when county councils are being contested. Some district councils follow the method of one-third of councillors retiring every year and elections for the full council every four years.

Chapter 7

1 It was reported by Rose that in 1979 7 per cent of the adult population in the UK could be called 'political activists' and 19 per cent of respondents admitted having 'a great deal of interest' in politics (Rose 1980). In our sample of the 1979 survey, 17 per cent of the respondents claimed to have attended political party meetings.

2 The involvement of ethnic minority individuals in election campaigns is so wide and frequent that it is not possible to present a national picture unless close monitoring is undertaken in very large parliamentary constituencies and local wards. However, it is true to say that ethnic minorities, wherever they live, have become an integral part of election campaigns.

3 The ethnic minority press coverage of the 1983 general election generally and of ethnic minority candidates and race and immigration issues in particular, was so extensive that it is not possible to include all those items here. However, those interested in this subject should see the relevant issues of ethnic minority papers. A list of the ethnic minority press published by the Commission for Racial Equality is a good guide in this context.

Chapter 8

1 Political parties are entitled to political broadcasts if their candidates number 50 or more.

2 In percentage terms the share of the National Front vote in Hackney South and Shoreditch constituency in the last three general elections was:

October 1974	1979	1983
%	%	%
9.4	7.6	1.6

This means there was a big decline in their vote in an area which was claimed by the National Front as one of its strongholds.

3 In Blackburn, which was seen as a stronghold of the National Front, its share of total votes was only 1.5 per cent. The National Front candidate, D. A. Riley,

received the same percentage vote (1.5 per cent) in the 1983 general election, which must be seen as a big rejection of this organization by the people of Blackburn.

4 The National Front share of the vote in Newham South in the October 1974 and 1979 general elections was 7.8 per cent and 6.2 per cent respectively. But the 1983 result shows that its share of the votes compared with 1979 was almost halved. In some other London constituencies the results were even worse for the National Front candidates at the 1983 general election.

Chapter 9

1 In March 1985, it was reported that 40 ethnic minority activists from the Handsworth Labour party in Birmingham (Part of the Perry Barr constituency) had resigned amidst allegations that some of them were also members of the Conservative party (*Birmingham Post*, 16 March 1985).

2 However, there has been one exception in the recent past where the leadership of Anglo-Jewry urged its members to vote for the three main political parties and, by doing this, vote against the National Front. Just before the general election, on 20 April 1979, the *Jewish Chronicle* published an article: 'How to Vote'. It suggested: 'Any vote cast for one of the established parties is a vote against the Front and, in this sense alone, might it be said that Jews are not only obliged to vote but have a vested collective interest, with the rest of civilised society in this country of ours, in exercising their franchise.' There are several examples of such an approach, including some supported by the Board of Deputies which has issued several leaflets against the National Front. In particular, the anti-National Front campaign waged by the Defence Committee of the Board of Deputies after 1974 'undoubtedly alerted the Jewish population to the dangers this party posed to Jews themselves. In fact, it might be said that an anti-National Front vote was orchestrated by Jewish leaders through appeals to Jews to exercise their franchise and thus reduce the National Front proportion of the total vote in national and local elections (Kosmin 1980).

3 In 1906, out of the 16 Jewish MPs, 12 were Liberals and four Conservatives. By 1945 the situation had changed dramatically; out of the 28 Jewish MPs in Parliament, 26 belonged to the Labour party, one was an Independent Conservative, and one was Communist. There was no Jewish Conservative or Liberal party MP. However, again in 1970, nine Jewish MPs got elected on the Conservative party ticket, while 31 reached the House of Commons for the Labour party. Only one Liberal party Jewish MP was elected in 1974.

4 Barry Kosmin has suggested that Jewish voting patterns are well integrated in the British political system: because of the 'considerable intergenerational social and spatial mobility among British Jews' (Kosmin 1980), their increasing support for the Conservative party is not surprising. The Jews have socioeconomic characteristics such as mostly middle class, higher owner-occupation rate, and self-employment well above the national average, which make them natural supporters of the Conservative party.

5 Its Chair is Clare Short (Lab.), MP for Birmingham Ladywood and its vice-chairs are: Geoffrey Lawler (Cons.), MP for Bradford North, and Robert Maclennan (SDP), MP for Caithness. The group has the support of over 70 MPs from the Labour, Conservative, Liberal/SDP Alliance parties.

6 However, in a recent speech Gerald Kaufman, the Shadow Home Secretary, said that 'instructions to immigration officers would be changed at once, and the law changed as soon as parliament time could be found.' He said that the Immigration Act 1971 was 'deliberately racially discriminating, seeking to exclude people with dark skins while allowing whites in' (*Daily Telegraph*, 15 April 1985: speech made at the Annual Conference of the United Kingdom Immigrants Advisory Service in Manchester on 13 April 1985).

Postscript

Councillor Mohammed Ajeeb (Lab.) was elected as the first Asian Lord Mayor in Britain for Bradford for 1985–86. Councillor Shreela Flather (Cons.) has been elected as Mayor of the Royal Borough of Windsor and Maidenhead for 1986–87, the first Asian woman in this country to take this office. The Labour party currently has an Afro-Caribbean, Lloyd Leon, as Mayor of Lambeth. Also the Labour party has had mayors of ethnic minority origin in Slough, and the London Boroughs of Brent, Hackney, and Hounslow.

Councillor Bernie Grant (Lab.) from Haringey is the first ethnic minority person to become the leader of a council in this country. He is also the prospective parliamentary candidate for Tottenham, a safe Labour seat. Merle Amory was elected the first ethnic minority woman leader of the Labour group in Brent.

The Labour party has so far selected nine ethnic minority prospective parliamentary candidates to contest the next election. Five of these will be contesting 'safe' or 'winnable' seats. However, one of these is not yet endorsed by the Labour NEC because, in defiance of party rules, black section members participated in the selection. Diane Abbott, Westminster councillor, is almost certain to become Britain's first ethnic minority woman to enter Parliament, from Hackney North, a safe Labour seat.

The debate about black sections goes on. At the Labour party conference in October 1985, the resolution for setting up black sections was defeated by approximately 5 to 1, though the black section lobby trebled its support compared with the voting at the 1984 conference. Also a resolution to demand the automatic short-listing of ethnic minority persons nominated for local or parliamentary elections was rejected by a much larger majority. Instead a recommendation of the Labour NEC for setting up a Black and Asian Advisory Committee was accepted (*Guardian*, 10 October 1985).

The main political parties have continued their efforts to attract ethnic minority electoral support. Some of their efforts are reflected in the selection of several ethnic minority candidates for the forthcoming local elections in May 1986. The Leader of the Liberal party, David Steel, has set up a Commission of Inquiry chaired by Councillor Mrs Zarbanoo Gifford, to look into the ethnic minority involvement in the Liberal party.   *February 1986*

Appendix: Ethnic minority population in selected parliamentary constituencies

Constituency	1981 census[1] %	1987 estimates[2] %
Brent South	45.7	55.6
Ealing Southall	43.7	53.2
Birmingham Ladywood	42.8	52.0
Birmingham Small Heath	38.8	46.8
Tottenham	37.5	45.3
Birmingham Sparkbrook	35.2	42.5
Newham North-West	32.7	39.3
Newham North-East	32.6	39.3
Hackney North and Stoke Newington	30.7	37.0
Brent East	29.9	36.6
Bradford West	27.0	32.5
Leyton	26.7	32.2
Leicester East	26.3	31.7
Leicester South	25.3	30.5
Vauxhall	25.1	30.3
Bethnal Green and Stepney	24.4	29.4
Hackney South and Shoreditch	24.4	29.4
Tooting	24.1	29.3
Norwood	23.4	28.2
Lewisham Deptford	23.4	28.2
Brent North	23.0	27.8
Croydon North-West	22.7	27.3
Battersea	21.6	26.0
Hornsey and Wood Green	21.3	25.7

Constituency	1981 census[1] %	1987 estimates[2] %
Warley East	21.2	25.6
Islington North	21.0	25.4
Slough	20.9	25.4
Peckham	20.6	24.8
Streatham	20.2	24.6
Ilford South	19.9	24.0
Feltham and Heston	19.6	23.6
Walthamstow	19.6	23.6
Hammersmith	18.2	22.0
Enfield Southgate	18.1	21.8
Wolverhampton South-East	17.9	21.7
Wolverhampton South-West	17.7	21.6
Derby South	17.3	20.8
Stretford	17.2	20.7
Dulwich	17.2	20.7
Edmonton	17.0	20.5
Harrow East	16.9	20.3
Finchley	16.4	20.0
Coventry North-East	16.3	20.0
Birmingham Perry Barr	16.0	19.3
Luton South	16.0	19.3
Bow and Poplar	15.4	18.5
Walsall South	15.1	18.2
Westminster North	15.0	18.2
Bradford North	15.0	18.1
Blackburn	14.8	17.9
Hendon South	14.8	17.8
Huddersfield	14.7	17.7
Ealing North	14.3	17.2
Ealing Acton	14.0	17.9
Brentford and Isleworth	13.7	16.5
Croydon North-East	13.4	16.1
Harrow West	13.3	16.0
Newham South	13.0	15.7
Manchester Gorton	12.4	15.0
Leicester West	12.3	15.0

Notes

1 *Parliamentary Constituency Monitors (1983 Boundaries)*: Census 1981, London: OPCS 1983.
2 These estimates also take into account: the NCWP population resident in non-private households, the UK-born persons of NCWP ethnic origin who head their households together with the other members of their households and an estimated average annual increase of about 2.5 per cent for the NCWP population. However, this method involves a small margin of error. Calculations for certain areas show that the NCWP population as presented in the table for 1987 is underestimated. For example, in some areas the average annual increase is estimated at more than 5 per cent (Tower Hamlets [6.3 per cent], Oldham [5.6 per cent], Rochdale [5.3 per cent], and so on).

References

Alderman, G. (1983) *The Jewish Community in British Politics*. Oxford: Clarendon Press.

Allen, S. (1971) *New Minorities Old Conflicts, Asian and West Indian Migrants in Britain*. New York: Random House.

Anwar, M. (1973) Pakistani Participation in the 1972 Rochdale By-Election. *New Community* II (4): 418–23.

—— (1974a) Pakistani Participation in the 1973 Rochdale Local Elections. *New Community* III (1–2).

—— (1974b) Pakistanis and Indians in the 1971 Census: Some Ambiguities. *New Community* III (4).

—— (1975) Asian Participation in the 1974 Autumn Election. *New Community* IV (3): 376–83.

—— (1976) *Between Two Cultures*. London: Community Relations Commission.

—— (1978) Much Ado About A Trickle (and Not Rights). *Impact International*, 12–25 May.

—— (1979a) Voting Patterns Among the Asians. In Claire Demouth (ed.) *Parties, Politics and the Asian Community*. London: National Association of Asian Youth.

—— (1979b) *The Myth of Return: Pakistanis in Britain*. London: Heinemann.

—— (1979c) British Voters Reject the National Front. *Impact International*, 27 July–9 August.

—— (1980a) *Votes and Policies*. London: Commission for Racial Equality.

—— (1980b) Pakistani Participation in British Elections. *Dawn*, 23 March.

—— (1981a) The Ethnic Vote: Mountains and Molehills. *New Community* IX (2): 281–83.

Anwar, M. (1981b) *Race Relations in 1981*. London: Commission for Racial Equality.

—— (1982a) Public Reactions to the Scarman Report. *New Community* X (3): 371–73.

—— (1982b) *Young People and the Job Market*. London: Commission for Racial Equality.

—— (1984a) *Ethnic Minorities and the 1983 General Election*. London: Commission for Racial Equality.

—— (1984b) *Muslims in Europe: Demographic, Social and Civic Situation*. Birmingham: Centre for the Study of Islam and Christian – Muslim Relations, Selly Oak Colleges.

Anwar, M. and Kohler, D. (1975) *Participation of Ethnic Minorities in the General Election, October 1974*. London: Community Relations Commission.

Benewick, R. (1972) *The Fascist Movement in Britain*. London: Allen Lane.

Billing, M. (1978) *Fascists: A Social Psychological View of the National Front*. London: Academic Press.

Black People's Conference (1979) *Black People's Manifesto*.

Bonham-Carter, M. (1979) *Comparative Approaches to the Resolution of Racial Conflict*. A Keynote Address delivered on the 15th Anniversary of the South African Institute of Race Relations.

Braham, P. (1982) *Migration and Settlement in Britain*. London: Oxford University Press.

Brittan, L. (1983) Speech made in Bradford.

—— (1984) Speech made in Brent.

Brockway, F. (1964) Why I Lost Eton and Slough. *Tribune*, 23 October.

Brown, C. (1984) *Black and White Britain*. London: Policies Studies Institute.

Butler, D. and Kavanagh, D. (1974) *The British General Election of February 1974*. London: Macmillan.

—— (1975) *The British General Election of October 1974*. London: Macmillan.

Butler, D. and Pinto-Duschinsky, M. (1971) *The British General Election of 1970*. London: Macmillan.

Butler, D. and Stokes, D. (1974) *Political Change in Britain*. London: Macmillan.

Cabinet Papers (1950) *Coloured People from British Colonial Territories*. CP (50) 113, May. London: Public Records Office.

—— (1951) *Immigration of British Subjects into the United Kingdom*. CP 128/44, February. London: Records Office.

Cavanagh, T. E. (1984) *The Impact of the Black Electorate*. Washington DC: Joint Center for Political Studies.

Commission for Racial Equality (1981–84) *Annual Reports*. London: CRE.

—— (1984) *Housing in Hackney*. London: CRE.

Community Relations Commission (1976) *Some of My Best Friends*. London: Community Relations Commission.

Conservative Party (1979 and 1983) *Conservative Party Manifestos*.

Crewe, I. (1983) Representation and the Ethnic Minorities. In Nathan Glazer and Ken Young (eds) *Ethnic Pluralism and Public Policy*. London: Heinemann Educational Books.

Crewe, I. and Sarlvik, B. (1977) Partisan Delignment in Britain 1964–74. *British Journal of Political Science* VII (2).

Crossman, R. (1975) *Diaries of a Cabinet Minister* Vol. 1. London: Hamish Hamilton & Jonathan Cape.

Deakin, N. (1970) *Colour, Citizenship and British Society*. London: Panther Books.

—— (ed.) (1965) *Colour and the British Electorate*. London: Pall Mall Press.

Deakin, N. and Bourne, J. (1970) Powell, the Minorities and the 1970 Election. *Political Quarterly* 41 (4).

Engels, F. (1952) *The Conditions of the Working Class in England in 1844*. London: George Allen & Unwin.

Fielding, N. (1981) *The National Front*. London: Routledge & Kegan Paul.

FitzGerald, M. (1983) *Ethnic Minorities and the 1983 General Election*. London: Runnymede Trust.

—— (1984) *Political Parties and Black People*. London: Runnymede Trust.

Foot, P. (1965) *Immigration and Race in British Politics*. Harmondsworth: Penguin.

Gray, P. E. and Gee, F. A. (1967) *Electoral Registration for Parliamentary Elections*. London: Government Social Survey.

Hanna, M. (1974) *The National Front and Other Right-Wing Organisations*. *New Community* III (1–2): 49–55.

Hansard. See relevant *Parliamentary Debates*.

Harris Research Centre (1983) *General Election 1983 Survey for LWT*.

Hatfield, M. (1978) *The House the Left Built: Inside Labour Policy Making 1970–75*. London: Gollancz.

HMSO (1977) *British Nationality Law. Discussion of Possible Changes*. London: HMSO.

Home Office (1975) *Racial Discrimination*. (White Paper) London: HMSO.

—— (1981) *Racial Attacks: Report of a Home Office Study*. London: HMSO.

—— (1985) *Control of Immigration: Statistics United Kingdom 1984*. London: HMSO.

Home Affairs Committee (1981) *Racial Disadvantage*. London: HMSO.

Husbands, C. (1975) The National Front: A Response to Crisis. *New Society*, 15 May.

—— (1983) *Racial Exclusionism and the City: the urban Support of the National Front*. London: George Allen & Unwin.

Isaac, J. (1954) *British Postwar Migration*. London: Cambridge University Press.

Jackson, J. A. (1963) *The Irish in Britain*. London: Routledge & Kegan Paul.

John D. W. (1969) *Indian Workers' Association in Britain*. London: Oxford University Press.

Katznelson, I. (1973) *Blackmen White Cities*. London: Oxford University Press.

Kosmin, B. (1980) Jewish voters in the United Kingdom: the Question of a Jewish vote. *Research Report No. 10*, London: Institute of Jewish Affairs.

Labour Party (1964, 1974, 1979, and 1983) *Labour Party Manifestos*.

—— (1980) Labour and the Black Electorate. A circular sent to CLPs.

—— (1984) Annual Party Conference Papers.

Labour Party Race Action Group (1979) Don't Take Black Voters for Granted. A circular sent to CLPs.

Lawrence, D. (1974) *Black Migrants: White Natives*. Cambridge: Cambridge University Press.

Layton-Henry, Z. (1978) The Tories in Two Minds Over Race. *New Society*, 25 September.

—— (1984) *The Politics of Race in Britain*. London: George Allen & Unwin.

Layton-Henry, Z. and Taylor, S. (1977) Race at the Polls. *New Society*, 25 August.

Layton-Henry, Z. and Taylor, S. (1978) Race and Politics: the Case of the Ladywood By-Election. *New Community* VI (1–2): 130–42.

Le Lohe, M. J. (1975) Participation in Elections by Asians in Bradford. In I. Crewe (ed.) *The Politics of Race*. London: Croom Helm.

Le Lohe, M. J. (1979) The Effect of the Presence of Immigrants upon the Local Political System in Bradford. In R. Miles and A. Phizacklea (eds) *Racism and Political Action*. London: Routledge & Kegan Paul.

—— (1982) *The Participation of the Ethnic Minorities in the British Political Process*. A report submitted to the Commission for Racial Equality.

—— (1983) Voters' Discrimination Against Asian and Black Candidates in the 1983 Election. *New Community* IX (1–2): 101–08.

—— (1984) *Ethnic Minority Participation in Local Elections*. Bradford: University of Bradford.

Le Lohe, M. J. and Goldman, A. (1969) Race in Local Politics: the Rochdale Central Ward Election of 1968. *Race* XI (4).

Leonard, R. L. (1968) *Elections in Britain*. London: D. van Nostrand Co.

Liberal Party (1979) *Liberal Party Manifesto*.

—— (1981a) *Nationality Law*. A document giving the Liberal party proposals.

—— (1981b) *Inner City Disturbances*. London.

—— (1982) *The Liberal Programme*. London.

Liberal Party/SDP Alliance (1983) Liberal/SDP Alliance Party Manifesto.

NOP (1978) Immigration and Race Relations. Political, Social and Economic Review 14.

Nugent, N. and King, R. (1977) *The British Right*. London: Saxon House.

Office of Population Censuses and Surveys (1983) *Census 1981: National Report, Great Britain*. London: HMSO.

—— (1983) *Parliamentary Constituency Monitors* 1–12. London: OPCS.

Patterson, S. (1965) *Dark Strangers*. Harmondsworth: Penguin.

—— (1969) *Immigrants in Industry 1960–67*. London: Oxford University Press.

Perriman, H. R. (ed.) (1975) *Britain at the Polls: The Parliamentary Elections of 1974*. Washington DC: American Institute for Public Policy Research.

Rex, J. and Tomlinson, S. (1979) *Colonial Immigrants in a British City*. London: Routledge & Kegan Paul.

Rose, E. J. B., Deakin, N., Abrahams, M., Jackson, V., Peston, M., Vanags, A. H., Cohen, B., Gaiskell, J., and Ward, P. (1969) *Colour and Citizenship*. London: Oxford University Press.

Rose, R. (1980) *Politics in England Today*. London: Faber & Faber.

Scarman, Lord (1981) *The Brixton Disorders April 10–12: Report of an Inquiry*. London: HMSO.

Scott, D. (1975) *The National Front in Local Politics*: Some Interpretations. In I. Crewe (ed.) *The Politics of Race*. London: Croom Helm.

Singh, R. (1979) The British Election and the Punjabi Press. *The Asian* II (2).

Spencer, R. (1970) The Minorities and the General Election 1970. *Race Today*, July.

Stokes, D. E. (1966) Spatial Models of Party Competition. In Angus Campbell *et al. Elections and the Political Order*. New York: John Wiley.

Studlar, D. (1978) Policy Voting in Britain: The Coloured Immigration Issue in the 1964, 1966 and 1970 General Elections. *American Political Science Review* 72: 46–72.

Studlar, D. and Layton-Henry, Z. (1984) *The Political Participation of Black and Asian Britons*. Working Paper No. 36. Department of Politics, University of Warwick.

Taylor, S. (1980) The Liberal Party and Immigration Control: a Case Study in Political Deviance. *New Community* VIII (1–2): 107–14.

—— (1982) *The National Front in English Politics*. London: Macmillan.

Thompson, E. P. (1968) *The Making of the English Working Class*. Harmondsworth: Penguin.

The Times (1983) *Guide to the House of Commons*. London: Times Books.

Todd, J. and Butcher, B. (1982) *Electoral Registration in 1981*. London: Office of Population Censuses and Surveys.

Troyna, B. (1982) Reporting the National Front: British Values Observed. In C. Husband (ed.) *Race in Britain*. London: Hutchinson.

United Nations Economic Commission for Europe (1979) *Labour Supply and Migration in Europe*. New York: United Nations.

Walker, M. (1977) *The National Front*. London: Fontana.

Name index

Subject index